CBW

Library of
Davidson College

Carnegie Commission on Higher Education
Sponsored Research Studies

EDUCATION AND EVANGELISM:
A PROFILE OF PROTESTANT COLLEGES
C. Robert Pace

PROFESSIONAL EDUCATION:
SOME NEW DIRECTIONS
Edgar H. Schein

THE NONPROFIT RESEARCH INSTITUTE:
ITS ORIGIN, OPERATION, PROBLEMS, AND PROSPECTS
Harold Orlans

THE INVISIBLE COLLEGES:
A PROFILE OF SMALL, PRIVATE COLLEGES WITH LIMITED RESOURCES
Alexander W. Astin and Calvin B. T. Lee

A DEGREE AND WHAT ELSE?:
CORRELATES AND CONSEQUENCES OF A COLLEGE EDUCATION
Stephen B. Withey, Jo Anne Coble, Gerald Gurin, John P. Robinson, Burkhard Strumpel, Elizabeth Keogh Taylor, and Arthur C. Wolfe

THE MULTICAMPUS UNIVERSITY:
A STUDY OF ACADEMIC GOVERNANCE
Eugene C. Lee and Frank M. Bowen

INSTITUTIONS IN TRANSITION:
A PROFILE OF CHANGE IN HIGHER EDUCATION
(INCORPORATING THE 1970 STATISTICAL REPORT)
Harold L. Hodgkinson

EFFICIENCY IN LIBERAL EDUCATION:
A STUDY OF COMPARATIVE INSTRUCTIONAL COSTS FOR DIFFERENT WAYS OF ORGANIZING TEACHING-LEARNING IN A LIBERAL ARTS COLLEGE
Howard R. Bowen and Gordon K. Douglass

CREDIT FOR COLLEGE:
PUBLIC POLICY FOR STUDENT LOANS
Robert W. Hartman

MODELS AND MAVERICKS:
A PROFILE OF PRIVATE LIBERAL ARTS COLLEGES
Morris T. Keeton

BETWEEN TWO WORLDS:
A PROFILE OF NEGRO HIGHER EDUCATION
Frank Bowles and Frank A. DeCosta

BREAKING THE ACCESS BARRIERS:
A PROFILE OF TWO-YEAR COLLEGES
Leland L. Medsker and Dale Tillery

ANY PERSON, ANY STUDY:
AN ESSAY ON HIGHER EDUCATION IN THE UNITED STATES
Eric Ashby

THE NEW DEPRESSION IN HIGHER EDUCATION:
A STUDY OF FINANCIAL CONDITIONS AT 41 COLLEGES AND UNIVERSITIES
Earl F. Cheit

FINANCING MEDICAL EDUCATION:
AN ANALYSIS OF ALTERNATIVE POLICIES AND MECHANISMS
Rashi Fein and Gerald I. Weber

HIGHER EDUCATION IN NINE COUNTRIES:
A COMPARATIVE STUDY OF COLLEGES AND UNIVERSITIES ABROAD
Barbara B. Burn, Philip G. Altbach, Clark Kerr, and James A. Perkins

BRIDGES TO UNDERSTANDING:
INTERNATIONAL PROGRAMS OF AMERICAN COLLEGES AND UNIVERSITIES
Irwin T. Sanders and Jennifer C. Ward

GRADUATE AND PROFESSIONAL EDUCATION 1980:
A SURVEY OF INSTITUTIONAL PLANS
Lewis B. Mayhew

THE AMERICAN COLLEGE AND AMERICAN CULTURE:
SOCIALIZATION AS A FUNCTION OF HIGHER EDUCATION
Oscar and Mary F. Handlin

RECENT ALUMNI AND HIGHER EDUCATION:
A SURVEY OF COLLEGE GRADUATES
Joe L. Spaeth and Andrew M. Greeley

CHANGE IN EDUCATIONAL POLICY:
SELF-STUDIES IN SELECTED COLLEGES AND UNIVERSITIES
Dwight R. Ladd

STATE OFFICIALS AND HIGHER EDUCATION:
A SURVEY OF THE OPINIONS AND EXPECTATIONS OF POLICY MAKERS IN NINE STATES
Heinz Eulau and Harold Quinley

ACADEMIC DEGREE STRUCTURES:
INNOVATIVE APPROACHES
PRINCIPLES OF REFORM IN DEGREE STRUCTURES IN THE UNITED STATES
Stephen H. Spurr

COLLEGES OF THE FORGOTTEN AMERICANS:
A PROFILE OF STATE COLLEGES AND REGIONAL UNIVERSITIES
E. Alden Dunham

FROM BACKWATER TO MAINSTREAM:
A PROFILE OF CATHOLIC HIGHER EDUCATION
Andrew M. Greeley

THE ECONOMICS OF THE MAJOR PRIVATE UNIVERSITIES
William G. Bowen
(Out of print, but available from University Microfilms.)

THE FINANCE OF HIGHER EDUCATION
Howard R. Bowen
(Out of print, but available from University Microfilms.)

ALTERNATIVE METHODS OF FEDERAL FUNDING FOR HIGHER EDUCATION
Ron Wolk

INVENTORY OF CURRENT RESEARCH ON HIGHER EDUCATION 1968
Dale M. Heckman and Warren Bryan Martin

The following technical reports are available from the Carnegie Commission on Higher Education, 1947 Center Street, Berkeley, California 94704.

RESOURCE USE IN HIGHER EDUCATION:
TRENDS IN OUTPUT AND INPUTS, 1930–1967
June O'Neill

TRENDS AND PROJECTIONS OF PHYSICIANS IN THE UNITED STATES 1967–2002
Mark S. Blumberg

MENTAL ABILITY AND HIGHER EDUCATIONAL ATTAINMENT IN THE 20TH CENTURY
Paul Taubman and Terence Wales

SOURCES OF FUNDS TO COLLEGES AND UNIVERSITIES
June O'Neill

MAY 1970:
THE CAMPUS AFTERMATH OF CAMBODIA AND KENT STATE
Richard E. Peterson and John A. Bilorusky

The following reprints are available from the Carnegie Commission on Higher Education, 1947 Center Street, Berkeley, California 94704.

ACCELERATED PROGRAMS OF MEDICAL EDUCATION, *by Mark S. Blumberg, reprinted from* JOURNAL OF MEDICAL EDUCATION, *vol. 46, no. 8, August 1971.*

SCIENTIFIC MANPOWER FOR 1970–1985, *by Allan M. Cartter, reprinted from* SCIENCE, *vol. 172, no. 3979, pp. 132–140, April 9, 1971.*

A NEW METHOD OF MEASURING STATES' HIGHER EDUCATION BURDEN, *by Neil Timm, reprinted from* THE JOURNAL OF HIGHER EDUCATION, *vol. 42, no. 1, pp. 27–33, January 1971.*

REGENT WATCHING, by Earl F. Cheit, reprinted from AGB REPORTS, vol. 13, no. 6, pp. 4–13, March 1971.*

COLLEGE GENERATIONS—FROM THE 1930s TO THE 1960s, by Seymour M. Lipset and Everett C. Ladd, Jr., reprinted from THE PUBLIC INTEREST, no. 25, Summer 1971.

AMERICAN SOCIAL SCIENTISTS AND THE GROWTH OF CAMPUS POLITICAL ACTIVISM IN THE 1960s, by Everett C. Ladd, Jr., and Seymour M. Lipset, reprinted from SOCIAL SCIENCES INFORMATION, vol. 10, no. 2, April 1971.

THE POLITICS OF AMERICAN POLITICAL SCIENTISTS, by Everett C. Ladd, Jr., and Seymour M. Lipset, reprinted from PS, vol. 4, no. 2, Spring 1971.*

THE DIVIDED PROFESSORIATE, by Seymour M. Lipset and Everett C. Ladd, Jr., reprinted from CHANGE, vol. 3, no. 3, pp. 54–60, May 1971.

JEWISH AND GENTILE ACADEMICS IN THE UNITED STATES: ACHIEVEMENTS, CULTURES AND POLITICS, by Seymour M. Lipset and Everett C. Ladd, Jr., reprinted from AMERICAN JEWISH YEAR BOOK, 1971.

THE UNHOLY ALLIANCE AGAINST THE CAMPUS, by Kenneth Keniston and Michael Lerner, reprinted from NEW YORK TIMES MAGAZINE, November 8, 1970.

PRECARIOUS PROFESSORS: NEW PATTERNS OF REPRESENTATION, by Joseph W. Garbarino, reprinted from INDUSTRIAL RELATIONS, vol. 10, no. 1, February 1971.

... AND WHAT PROFESSORS THINK: ABOUT STUDENT PROTEST AND MANNERS, MORALS, POLITICS, AND CHAOS ON THE CAMPUS, by Seymour Martin Lipset and Everett C. Ladd, Jr., reprinted from PSYCHOLOGY TODAY, November 1970.*

DEMAND AND SUPPLY IN U.S. HIGHER EDUCATION: A PROGRESS REPORT, by Roy Radner and Leonard S. Miller, reprinted from AMERICAN ECONOMIC REVIEW, May 1970.*

RESOURCES FOR HIGHER EDUCATION: AN ECONOMIST'S VIEW, by Theodore W. Schultz, reprinted from JOURNAL OF POLITICAL ECONOMY, vol. 76, no. 3, University of Chicago, May/June 1968.*

INDUSTRIAL RELATIONS AND UNIVERSITY RELATIONS, by Clark Kerr, reprinted from PROCEEDINGS OF THE 21ST ANNUAL WINTER MEETING OF THE INDUSTRIAL RELATIONS RESEARCH ASSOCIATION, pp. 15–25.*

NEW CHALLENGES TO THE COLLEGE AND UNIVERSITY, by Clark Kerr, reprinted from Kermit Gordon (ed.), AGENDA FOR THE NATION, The Brookings Institution, Washington, D.C., 1968.*

PRESIDENTIAL DISCONTENT, by Clark Kerr, reprinted from David C. Nichols (ed.), PERSPECTIVES ON CAMPUS TENSIONS: PAPERS PREPARED FOR THE SPECIAL COMMITTEE ON CAMPUS TENSIONS, *American Council on Education, Washington, D.C., September 1970.*

STUDENT PROTEST—AN INSTITUTIONAL AND NATIONAL PROFILE, by Harold Hodgkinson, reprinted from THE RECORD, *vol. 71, no. 4, May 1970.*

WHAT'S BUGGING THE STUDENTS?, by Kenneth Keniston, reprinted from EDUCATIONAL RECORD, *American Council on Education, Washington, D.C., Spring 1970.*

THE POLITICS OF ACADEMIA, by Seymour Martin Lipset, reprinted from David C. Nichols (ed.), PERSPECTIVES ON CAMPUS TENSIONS: PAPERS PREPARED FOR THE SPECIAL COMMITTEE ON CAMPUS TENSIONS, *American Council on Education, Washington, D.C., September 1970.*

INTERNATIONAL PROGRAMS OF U.S. COLLEGES AND UNIVERSITIES: PRIORITIES FOR THE SEVENTIES, *by James A. Perkins, reprinted by permission of the International Council for Educational Development, Occasional paper no. 1, July 1971.*

FACULTY UNIONISM: FROM THEORY TO PRACTICE, by Joseph W. Garbarino, reprinted from INDUSTRIAL RELATIONS, *vol. 11, no. 1, pp. 1–17, February 1972.*

*The Commission's stock of this reprint has been exhausted.

*Education
and Evangelism*

Education and Evangelism

A PROFILE OF PROTESTANT COLLEGES

by *C. Robert Pace*

Professor of Higher Education
University of California, Los Angeles

Eleventh of a Series of Profiles Sponsored by
The Carnegie Commission on Higher Education

MCGRAW-HILL BOOK COMPANY

New York   St. Louis   San Francisco   Düsseldorf
London   Sydney   Toronto   Mexico   Panama
Johannesburg   Kuala Lumpur   Montreal
New Delhi   Rio de Janeiro   Singapore

The Carnegie Commission on Higher Education, 1947 Center Street, Berkeley, California 94704, has sponsored preparation of this profile as a part of a continuing effort to obtain and present significant information for public discussion. The views expressed are those of the author.

EDUCATION AND EVANGELISM
A Profile of Protestant Colleges

Copyright © 1972 by The Carnegie Foundation for the Advancement of Teaching. All rights reserved. Printed in the United States of America.

Library of Congress Cataloging in Publication Data

Pace, Charles Robert, date
 Education and evangelism.

"Eleventh of a series of profiles sponsored by the Carnegie Commission on Higher Education."
 Bibliography: p.
 1. Church colleges—U.S. I. Carnegie Commission on Higher Education. II. Title.

LC383.P28   377'.8   70-39711
ISBN 0-07-010045-4

123456789MAMM798765432

Contents

Foreword, xi

Acknowledgments, xv

1 *Introduction*, 1

2 *The Heritage*, 9

3 *The Environment*, 17
   Differences between mainline and evangelical colleges ▪ Differences related to strength of church connections ▪ A diagnostic look at specific characteristics

4 *The Graduates*, 47
   Estimates of educational benefits ▪ Involvement in current affairs ▪ Attitudes about social issues ▪ Personal traits and status ▪ Some personal expressions

5 *The Students*, 73
   Progress toward the attainment of educational benefits ▪ Activities and interests ▪ Attitudes toward social change ▪ Personal traits and status ▪ Some personal expressions

6 *Impressions and Thoughts*, 95
   Impressions ▪ Thoughts

References, 109

Appendix A: CUES, 111

Appendix B: Activity Scales from the Alumni Survey Questionnaire, 117

Index, 121

Foreword

One of the ongoing efforts of the Carnegie Commission on Higher Education has been the development of a general overview of America's total system of colleges and universities. Our approach has been to ask experienced observers to prepare profiles of the most significant components of the system, allowing each segment to fall into place as the complete design unfolds. The first segment was Andrew Greeley's profile of the Catholic colleges and universities of America. Subsequently, segments on state colleges and universities, community colleges, liberal arts colleges, black colleges, and the multicampus universities expanded the presentation. Depth has been provided by description of certain functions, such as international education, and by profiles of institutions undergoing change.

This profile by C. Robert Pace elaborates on many of the components already completed. The Protestant colleges of America are, in many respects, subgroups of the liberal arts colleges discussed for us by Morris Keeton in *Models and Mavericks.* Some of them have characteristics that match the small colleges with limited resources described for this series by Alexander Astin and Calvin B. T. Lee.

Unlike most of the profiles that precede it, *Education and Evangelism* tends to be intensive rather than extensive in its analysis. It is concerned less with size, structure, and financial support—characteristics in which they are much like liberal arts colleges generally—than it is with the implications of Protestant association to the character and environment of the Protestant colleges.

Professor Pace estimates that there are between 450 and 600 colleges and universities in the United States that have an association with Protestant Christianity. Among them are four major types:

1   Institutions that had Protestant roots but are no longer Protestant in any legal sense
2   Colleges that remain nominally related to Protestantism but are probably on the verge of disengagement
3   Colleges established by major Protestant denominations and which retain a connection with the church
4   Colleges associated with the evangelical, fundamentalist, and interdenominational Christian churches

Using data from three previous studies, Professor Pace concentrates on 88 representative institutions. In general, he finds them to be friendly, supportive, and congenial—characteristics Andrew Greeley found in the Catholic colleges.

The institutions he regards as "mainline Protestant" (those in the third type described above) have students very much like colleges generally. In fact, at such institutions decreasing numbers of students identify themselves as "Protestant," listing their preferences instead as "no definite beliefs" or "no formal religion."

The most distinctive Protestant colleges are those associated with evangelical or fundamentalist churches. The scholarship and awareness of their students is about the same as that for the mainline Protestant colleges, but they are more friendly and supportive, and score very high on measures of general decorum and regard for rules. They also have a high concern for leadership and encourage consistent effort toward pragmatic ends. The attitudes of their students often parallel those of their alumni and, significantly, their students still overwhelmingly identify themselves as Protestant.

Pace finds the evangelical-fundamentalist colleges in some ways outside the mainstream of social change, at least as it is understood by students in the nation's colleges and universities. Yet, because of the strong assistance they receive from those who financially and spiritually support their educational philosophy, their future looks secure. So, ironically, does the future of colleges with very loose ties to their supporting church, and which are in some ways more liberal than avowedly nonsectarian liberal arts colleges. Perhaps in greatest difficulty are those mainline denominational colleges that do not now seem committed to either a strong religious philosophy or a strong academic program.

The profile that Professor Pace has developed sheds helpful light on an important segment of higher education.

Clark Kerr
Chairman
The Carnegie Commission
on Higher Education

April 1972

Acknowledgments

The major parts of this book have drawn upon ongoing research studies in the higher education program, Graduate School of Education, University of California at Los Angeles.

The historical information and comment in Chapter 2, "The Heritage," comes from a doctoral dissertation by James Edwin Orr (1971). Dr. Orr, himself a world renowned evangelist as well as a historian, has provided remarkable documentation of evangelical awakenings in the United States and elsewhere. One special contribution of his research has been to show the extent to which such awakenings have been occurring on college campuses during the twentieth century. It was rewarding for me, both professionally and personally, to have served as Dr. Orr's sponsor at UCLA. Most of Chapter 2, except for the last two or three pages, is put together verbatim, or close to verbatim, from Dr. Orr's book. The language is his; the selection of sentences is mine. I am grateful for his permission to present this précis of his research.

The data in Chapter 3, "The Environment," come from the use of an instrument of mine, College and University Environment Scales (CUES), published by Educational Testing Service (ETS).[1] When a college employs the scoring service at ETS to tabulate and report the responses of its students on CUES, a copy of the printout is sent to the author. Thus I am indebted to ETS for my accumulating CUES reports from Protestant colleges. The national norm, or baseline population, that is used in interpreting CUES scores was developed under a research contract with the United States Office of Education (USOE) (Pace, 1967).

---

[1] See Pace (1969*a*).

The data in Chapters 4 and 5 on "The Graduates" and "The Students" come from a national survey of college students, college alumni, and college environments conducted within the Center for the Study of Evaluation, Graduate School of Education, UCLA.[2] The center is one of nine research and development centers in the field of education funded by USOE. Projects concerned with evaluation in higher education have been part of the center's overall program since its beginning in 1966. The fact that we had already collected the data from some 88 participating colleges enabled us to look at a special segment of those colleges (Protestant) in relation to a national baseline composed of thousands of students and alumni from all sorts of colleges and universities.

My research assistant throughout the preparation of this book was Sonja Jacobson (Mrs. James Mahoney). She located references, abstracted reports, collected materials, got data on and off the computer, and put together many tabulations of the student, alumni, and environment data. These days, no survey research project can even get off the ground without a good research assistant. Others in our office whose work and willingness have been much appreciated include Mary Milne, research assistant; Barbara Vizents, secretary; and Barbara Dorf, clerk. My faculty colleague, James W. Trent, although not directly involved in the Protestant college study, is jointly responsible with me for the national evaluation of higher education and other projects in higher education within the Center for the Study of Evaluation. Putting the national data in usable shape, preparing reports for each institution of its own data, and developing normative reports based on the data from all of the participating colleges involved the efforts of programmers Michael Huberman and Donald Long and of research educationist Ann Morey. If the data from the national study had not been accessible, we would not have had access to the data from the Protestant colleges that were part of that larger research inquiry. A special study of the write-in comments at the end of the alumni questionnaire was started by June Warren, and I have used some of those comments.

My visits to a number of Protestant colleges were enlightening,

---

[2] See *Alumni Survey* (1969) and *College Students Survey* (1969).

thanks to the cordiality and frankness of presidents, academic deans, financial officers, admissions officers, student personnel deans, directors of chapel programs, and others with whom I talked. They, of course, are not responsible for my impressions, my biases, or my memories.

CRP

1. *Introduction*

What is a Protestant college? To this short, direct question there should be an equally direct answer. But there is not. From John Harvard to Billy Graham's latest crusade, Protestants have established well over 1,000 colleges. Some of them have not survived. Others have been transformed into private nonsectarian institutions, and some have even become state universities. Among those that have technically disengaged from a Protestant denomination, some still retain a Christian emphasis or recognition — through weekly chapel services or required courses in religion or philosophy — and thus have a Protestant character if not a legal affiliation with a denomination. No one would mistake them for Catholic colleges or Jewish colleges, or state colleges or state universities. Some colleges are also strongly evangelical or fundamentalist but are classified in directories or by the U.S. Office of Education's National Center for Educational Statistics as private or nonsectarian. The classification is literally correct but totally false in spirit, for these colleges are 100 percent Protestant. They are classified as nonsectarian simply because they are not connected with a particular denomination. So a Protestant college is not necessarily a denominational college; it may be one that relates itself to all evangelical Christianity.

The most recent and thorough study of church-sponsored higher education was published in 1966 by the Danforth Foundation. (Pattillo & MacKenzie, 1966) The directors of the study wrote to the presidents of the 1,189 institutions that were at that time listed as private rather than public. From their replies they classified 817 as church-related, another 18 as religious but not connected with a particular church, and 354 as independent of any religious identification. Of the total number, 339 were then Catholic institutions. Thus, barring a few possible exceptions, it seems plausible to estimate that there are now about 450 to 600 colleges associated with Protestant Christianity. Our use of a general rather than a precise number is owing to the fact that we have not attempted to take a census, for the number of colleges is constantly changing. For example, just within the 25 years since the end of World War II more than 100 Bible colleges or institutes have been established in the United States. Some of these have become liberal arts colleges and others have similarities to liberal arts colleges. Moreover, various evangelical and fundamentalist Protestant groups have been particularly active within the past few years in establishing new colleges. Keeping track of new Christian colleges is as difficult as keeping track of new public junior colleges—especially in California.

One might put Protestant colleges into four categories today. First, there are hundreds of great universities and small colleges that had Protestant roots but are no longer Protestant in any legal sense. One has to remember that throughout the seventeenth, eighteenth, and nineteenth centuries most colleges in the United States were founded by Christian groups, not by the state or by private nonreligious groups. Among these universities one would have to list most of the famous Ivy League institutions and such other major universities as Boston University, Syracuse, Northwestern, Chicago, Southern California, Duke, Wake Forest, Southern Methodist, Texas Christian, Baylor, and many others. Some still retain their religious connection, but most do not. Many liberal arts colleges are also in this category. Then, there is a group of colleges still nominally related to Protestantism but probably on the verge of disengagement; or if not actual disengagement, then their Christian heritage is a conversational topic limited to members of the college family and rarely discussed in public. The third and largest group of currently active and acknowledged church-sponsored colleges includes those that were established by some of the major Protestant denominations and still retain a connection with the church—Presbyterian, Methodist, Baptist, Lutheran, and others. At the time of the establishment of these colleges these denominations were strongly evangelical, but are not so today, or at least are not considered so by the groups that clearly identify themselves as fundamentalist and evangelical. The fourth group consists of colleges associated with the evangelical, fundamentalist, and interdenominational Christian churches. This is the fastest-growing group, a fact about which we shall comment later.

Our study is not a new survey specifically made for the Carnegie Commission but is a study based upon data we had already collected for other purposes, segments of which seemed particularly relevant to the study of Protestant colleges. If in the previous paragraphs we have tended, perhaps, to minimize the virtues of totally complete and accurate accounting, we have done so for the simple reason that we are in no position to make such an accounting. Nor do we think it is crucial to our inquiry or to our conclusions that everyone agree with us about the way we categorize our colleges. The underlying condition is one of historical development and current change. The terrain we are dealing with is drifting.

The colleges from which we have data, and which therefore constitute the base for our profile, were not specifically selected to provide a sample. They were not picked at random from some specified total population of colleges. We identify the names of the colleges so the reader can judge whether they are reasonable examples. Two major data sources merit at least a brief description. The chapter "The Environment" is based on an accumulation of reports from colleges that, on their own initiative, decided to administer the College and University Environment Scales (CUES) to some sample of their students within the past several years. We went through the files to identify all the Protestant colleges. We further limited the number of colleges subsequently used to those whose reports were based on what we regarded as a good cross section of students who had been in the college long enough to become familiar with its environment. As we explain in a later chapter, the instrument is a means of getting the collective perception of students about what is characteristic of their college. Reports based on some special group of students — such as women only, rather than a cross section of both men and women — were not used; nor did we use reports based on the perceptions of freshmen or others who had not yet spent at least a year at the college. Typically, the reports about a college are based on the consensus of about 100 student reporters. In some cases the number of reporters is much larger, and in a few of the small colleges the number is as low as 50.

The other major data source is examined in the chapters "The Graduates" and "The Students." These data come from three nationwide evaluation surveys initiated and carried out through the Center for the Study of Evaluation in the Graduate School of Education at UCLA. The data were collected during 1969 from samples of alumni (class of 1950) and samples of upperclassmen and freshmen and involved a total of 88 colleges and universities, some of which participated in all three surveys. At each college and university, the student groups and the alumni were random samples or a reasonably good approximation of a probability sample. The institutions, however, were not randomly chosen; they were purposefully selected as examples of different types of institutions. The total set of institutions represents what we have characterized elsewhere as a national baseline—important categories of institutions chosen in a manner analogous to the purposeful selection of stocks (rails, utilities, etc.) that make up the Dow-Jones industrial index.

We think of this profile of Protestant colleges as an exploratory and descriptive study. It is not a hypothesis-testing research project, nor is it an effort to explain or demonstrate cause and effect after the manner of experimental science. Partly to emphasize the descriptive nature of our orientation we have limited our tabulations and comparisons to simple percentages. We have avoided even the simplest statistics of means and standard deviations. We do not even talk about "significant differences" between percentages, for even that assumes probability samples. Instead, we quite arbitrarily refer to noticeable differences, to dominant trend lines, and to such other characterizations as seem to us both reasonable and meaningful in describing our data.

Just as proper statisticians are consistent about applying their arbitrary standards, so are we about applying ours. When a percentage characterizing some subgroup (students at evangelical colleges, for example) is within 5 percentage points above or below our national baseline group, we describe the subgroup as being similar to the larger group. Deviations greater than 5 percentage points are called noticeable differences, or, depending on their magnitude, are characterized as obvious, large, or substantial, or are described by another term suitable to the case. When we are comparing different groups of Protestant colleges, looking for trends or noting the magnitude of a difference between the highest and lowest group, we look for differences that are larger than 10 percentage points before we regard them as worthy of note. The standards we are using are more conservative (i.e., more rigorous) than the conventional ones. Differences between percentages of the magnitude we have noted would always be statistically significant if they were based on probability samples as large as ours.

Our profile begins with a reminder of the heritage of Protestant higher education, noting especially the role of evangelical Christianity in the establishment of colleges and pointing out that this missionary spirit still permeates the atmosphere of many Protestant college campuses.

As we explore the characteristics of Protestant college environments, as perceived by the students who live in them, we find that the more evangelical and fundamentalist institutions differ markedly in some respects from other Protestant colleges as well as from liberal arts colleges in general. Our data come from 50 colleges related to mainline Protestant denominations and from 30 colleges related to more evangelical or fundamentalist groups. This data base is, we believe, quite adequate to write with some authority about different campus environments.

State distribution of colleges included in the profile

State	Distribution	State	Distribution
Alabama	1	New Jersey	1
Arkansas	1	New York	4
California	4	North Carolina	3
Florida	2	Ohio	7
Illinois	9	Oklahoma	1
Indiana	10	Oregon	3
Iowa	5	Pennsylvania	10
Kansas	1	Rhode Island	1
Maine	1	South Carolina	2
Maryland	1	Tennessee	3
Massachusetts	1	Texas	1
Michigan	3	Virginia	4
Minnesota	2	Washington	2
Missouri	2	Wisconsin	3

When we examine the alumni and the current students at some of these colleges, our data base shrinks to 19 for the alumni survey and to 16 for the study of upperclassmen. And when we further divide it into segments for the purpose of trying to find differences between evangelical or fundamentalist colleges and other Protestant colleges we are comparing groups at four or five evangelical-fundamentalist colleges with groups at nine or eleven mainline denominational colleges, and with groups at three colleges that we describe as Protestant-independent. Since approximately 100 students or alumni are sampled at any one college, the comparisons between groups are of the magnitude of 400–500 versus 900–1100 versus 300 people; but it is important, indeed crucial, in drawing conclusions with at least a moderate degree of plausibility to know whether the colleges are reasonably representative. Fortunately, they are. In most cases, we had scores on the College and University Environment Scales so that we could compare these scores with the composite scores of the much larger sets of colleges. The resemblance was almost perfect. On one dimension, propriety, the composite score for the small set of three Protestant-independent colleges was lower than that for its larger relevant comparison group. Since we are comparing three sets of colleges on each of five dimensions, there are 15 possible points of difference. Fourteen of these potential points of difference were so small that they could be described as "chance variations." Therefore, the smaller sets of colleges whose alumni and students we examine have environments similar to the larger sets of colleges that they should resemble.

Regional distribution of colleges included in the profile

Region	Distribution
Northeast (north of the District of Columbia to Maine and including New York and Pennsylvania)	19
South (south of the District of Columbia and west including Texas and Oklahoma)	18
Midwest (from Ohio to the Dakotas and south to Missouri and Kansas)	42
Mountain and Far West (from Montana to New Mexico and west)	9
	88

There are in total 88 colleges whose environments, students, or alumni we have examined in our profile. Most of these colleges are in small towns rather than in major cities. Two are in the greater Los Angeles area, and one each in Seattle, Indianapolis, Birmingham, and St. Paul. Thirteen others are located in cities of more moderate size, such as Little Rock, Portland (Oregon),

Bethlehem, Raleigh, and Springfield (Ohio). This leaves the vast majority of colleges in much smaller communities, such as Ripon, Wisconsin; Selinsgrove, Pennsylvania; Decorah, Iowa; Lynchburg, Virginia, and so on.

Most of the colleges are also small, but that is typical of liberal arts colleges. Of the 88 colleges, 33 have enrollments of fewer than 1,000 students; 15 of these 33 we have characterized as evangelical-fundamentalist. Geographically, the colleges are in 28 different states, with the largest number in the Midwest.

Distribution of enrollments of colleges included in the profile

Enrollment	Distribution
Under 1,000	33
1,000–1,999	41
2,000 and higher	14
	88

Two of the colleges are men's colleges, four are women's colleges, and two are classified as coordinate. The remaining 80 are coeducational. At the 19 coeducational colleges we studied most intensively the number of men and women is about equally divided, with slightly more women than men in the entering classes but slightly more men than women in the graduating classes.

In the 11 mainline denominational colleges in our national study, and averaging the reports of freshman and upperclassman samples, we found that 43 percent of the fathers and 31 percent of the mothers of the present students were college graduates. In the five more evangelical-fundamentalist colleges, the corresponding figures were 27 percent and 18 percent.

In subsequent chapters we shall be describing other differences among these colleges. We will also be noting the differences in the kinds of educational objectives that students and alumni of these colleges feel they have achieved—differences in the extent of their involvement in various sorts of activities, and differences in some of their values and viewpoints, personalities and politics.

Finally, having exhausted the empirical data that we could relate to our profile of Protestant colleges, we conclude with some observations based on visits to various campuses and with some thoughts about higher education today and tomorrow, about piety and politics, and about education and evangelism.

2. The Heritage

Evangelical Christianity was one of the major forces in the development of higher education in America and, indeed, in the spread of education throughout the world.[1] The American colonies were a refuge for persecuted Puritans. John Harvard, a Puritan landowner who bequeathed a sum of money toward the pious work of building a college, became the pastor of the Congregational Church in Charlestown, Massachusetts. The College of William and Mary was established with the avowed purpose of furnishing a seminary for ministers of the gospel and for training youth in good manners.

Out of the evangelical revival of the eighteenth century, first with Griffith Jones in Wales and later with the powerful preaching of George Whitefield and John Wesley, came a movement to develop schools for the illiterate and the poor. George Whitefield's visits to Philadelphia led to the founding of the University of Pennsylvania. A statue of this famous revivalist, unveiled on the Penn campus in 1914, paid tribute to him as the "inspirer and original trustee" of the university. William Tennent, an Ulsterman who came to Pennsylvania and became minister of a Presbyterian church in 1726, taught groups of young men in a log cabin school. Many of the "log college" graduates established other log colleges from which came new educational leaders. Among them was the first president of the College of New Jersey, which was founded to succeed Tennent's school and later was moved to the town of Princeton. Trinity Church in New York contributed a parcel of land to the establishment of King's College, which in due course became Columbia University. The Dutch

---

[1] The first segment of this chapter is drawn entirely, and for the most part verbatim, from portions of Orr (1971).

Reformed founded Queens College in New Brunswick, New Jersey, which continued as Rutgers University and is now the State University. Congregationalists founded Dartmouth College. Baptists opened Brown University, first known as Rhode Island College. Thus, far from being anti-intellectual, evangelism provoked educational enterprise.

From a Christian perspective, there was a general decline in morals and religion in the latter part of the the eighteenth century. The society was unsettled by a long war and a revolution, by the self-assertive feelings that accompanied independence, by the lure of the Western frontier and the breakup of family and church relationships due to migration, and by the strong influence of militant French infidelity. The bitter writings of Thomas Paine and the gentler ones of Thomas Jefferson both lent aid to the spread of a kind of deism and unbelief and to the work of skeptics, political radicals, and the French revolutionists. Timothy Dwight described college students:

Youths . . . with strong passions and feeble principles . . . delighted in the prospect of unrestrained gratification . . . and became enamored with the new doctrines . . . Striplings scarcely fledged suddenly found that the world had been enveloped in general darkness through the long succession of preceding ages, and that the light of human wisdom had just begun to dawn upon the human race.

Lyman Beecher, a sophomore at Yale in 1795, wrote:

College was in a most ungodly state. The college church was almost extinct. Most of the students were skeptical and rowdies were plenty. Wine and liquors were kept in many rooms; intemperance, profanity, gambling, and licentiousness were common. . . .

The colleges were seedbeds of infidelity. An anti-church play was featured at Dartmouth. Students at Williams conducted a mock celebration of Holy Communion. When the dean at Princeton opened the chapel Bible to read, a pack of playing cards fell out, some radical having cut a rectangle out of each page to accommodate the pack. Christians were so unpopular that they met in secret and kept their minutes in code. Students disrupted worship services with profanity, burned the Bible, burned down buildings, and forced the resignation of college presidents. The two largest denominations, the Methodists and Baptists, were losing more members than they were gaining. The Episcopal Bishop of New York quit functioning for lack of duties. Chief Justice Marshall wrote to Bishop Madison of Virginia declaring that the church was too far gone ever to be redeemed.

But then, around the beginning of the nineteenth century there was a spiritual awakening—both in Europe and in America. In the colleges, students took the initiative in forming new societies committed to prayer and fellowship, though at first secretly for fear of disturbance from the unpenitent. Timothy Dwight, who became president of Yale in 1795, exhorted the students to embrace Christianity. In 1802 a third of the students made professions of faith. Amherst, Dartmouth, Princeton, Williams, and other colleges reported student conversions. Dynamic Christian leaders became college presidents and professors. Campus prayer days became common. Collegiate awakenings and evangelical religion supplied the principal impetus for the creation of many new colleges. Between 1807 and 1827, 17 theological schools were founded. In Ohio, the Baptists founded Denison; the Congregationalists, Oberlin and Western Reserve; the Disciples, Antioch and Hiram; the Episcopalians, Kenyon; the Lutherans, Wittenberg; the Methodists, Ohio Wesleyan, Baldwin-Wallace, and Mount Union; the Presbyterians, Franklin and Muskingum; the Reformed, Heidelberg; and the United Brethren, Otterbein. Of 180 denominational colleges in the West in 1860, 144 or so were founded and maintained by the more evangelistic denominations.

By the middle of the nineteenth century, however, it was evident that the series of awakenings on college campuses had run its course. Reaction to evangelical religion found expression in the rise of Greek-letter fraternities, which offered escape from the collegiate regimen, which began with prayers before dawn and ended with prayers after dark. In society at large zeal was devoted to the accumulation of wealth and to passionate contention over the question of slavery. Moreover, the emerging state universities and secularized private colleges were officially neutral toward evangelism. Not only was the expectation of evangelical awakenings thereby lessened, but their realization was made even more unlikely by a widespread student revolt against compulsory chapel. Communal worship was at the heart of the evangelical community. With the passing of compulsory chapel, the likelihood of reaching the whole community in evangelistic ministry also passed.

Then, in 1858, a great nationwide religious awakening started whose beginnings have been traced to prayer meetings held in New York City in September 1857. The prayer meetings increased during the autumn and winter. Church after church was opened and filled at the noon hour. Then crowds also filled the theaters. Some historians have referred to the awakening of 1858 as the bank-panic revival; but both the intercessory and the evangelistic phases of the movement had begun before, or were independent of, the bank panic of 1857. No great religious awakening followed the bank panic of 1837, nor did any follow the collapse of 1929. The phenomena of the packed churches and the startling conversions occurred everywhere. Every denomination was affected. The Young Men's Christian Association took a leading part, for the movement was primarily a lay effort. Awakenings occurred in most of the colleges, beginning as meetings for prayer and continuing as manifestations of repentance, confession, and restitution. No single evangelist was responsible, nor did visiting clergy initiate the campus movements. The biggest single factor was the wave of services of intercession that spread to all the cities and towns in the country.

In October of 1858 students at the University of Virginia organized a YMCA, the first of a widespread movement establishing College YMCAs to meet student needs on secularized campuses. Ultimately these associations became the main vehicle of Christian witness in American colleges. At the University of Michigan the awakening led to the foundation of a Student Christian Association, while in many other colleges the graduating classes had a record number of candidates for the Christian ministry.

At the end of the eighteenth century, evangelical Christianity influenced a tiny part of the population of the world. But, in the nineteenth century, evangelical missionaries, impelled by the great awakenings, not only planted churches in Africa, Asia, and Latin America, but also profoundly influenced the course of education throughout the world, in some places playing a major role in the founding of educational systems.

Although the twentieth century dawned without mass premonition of disasters, either of war or of revolution, the new century was spontaneously greeted by prayer meetings entreating another visitation of the Spirit. The next 15 years proved to be years of great spiritual awakening around the world. The greatest movement was the Welsh revival of 1904, whose leading figure was a young student, Evan Roberts. Within three months from the time Roberts began preaching, a hundred thousand converts had been added to the churches of Wales, keeping them crowded on weeknights as well as on Sundays. Unprogrammed meetings were common, with anyone moved by the Spirit taking part. There was such an improvement in public morals that local authorities met to discuss what to do with the police forces, which were unemployed because of the revival. Drunkenness was so reduced that a wave of bankruptcies swept the taverns. Profanity was curbed, until it was said that the pit-ponies in the mines could not understand their orders.

The awakening spread to England, Scotland, Norway, Germany, Holland, Switzerland, Australia, New Zealand, South Africa, and America. In America, the Methodists and the Baptists reported a doubling of new memberships in 1905. The movement affected not only Christian colleges but state universities and secularized colleges as well. The World's Student Christian Federation declared February 12, 1905 as a Universal Day of Prayer for Students. In response, prayer groups met in college after college.

The mainspring of the continuing influence of the 1905 awakening was the voluntary Bible class on campus. And one of the products of the awakening was a veritable torrent of thousands of missionaries for overseas service. Among these missionaries was Dr. E. Stanley Jones, who became the best-known missionary to India in the twentieth century.

After World War I a polarization developed among Protestants between the so-called modernists and the fundamentalists. The social gospel came to dominate denominational leadership, making the social work of the gospel the primary message of the church. The fundamentalist was strong in conventional evangelism, the winning of men to personal faith in Christ, but often weak in social action. When leadership of the YMCA was taken by the modernists, the dissatisfied evangelists began to organize other campus fellowships, among them the Student Foreign Missions Fellowship and the Inter-Varsity Christian Fellowship.

Wheaton College in Illinois, where a significant revival had occurred in 1936, experienced another awakening in 1943. All classes were suspended for a day of prayer. The president of the student council was a young North Carolinian named William

Franklin Graham, who many years afterward recalled being deeply moved by that experience. More than 40 seniors went into mission fields. The war years saw the rise of a movement aimed at reaching teenagers whose fathers and brothers were serving in the Armed Forces and two Wheaton graduates took over the direction of this rapidly expanding movement—Youth for Christ. In a short time the movement was operating in 400 cities and Billy Graham became the leading Youth for Christ evangelist.

In 1949 and 1950 there were new stirrings of revival. A remarkable awakening occurred at Bethel College and Seminary in St Paul. Wheaton College, Asbury, Seattle Pacific, and Baylor were among the scores of colleges affected by subsequent awakenings During the school year of 1950-51, a year of widespread evangelism, the Campus Crusade for Christ was organized. Thousands heard the message of Billy Graham during the next 20 years— including multitudes of students at Minnesota, Michigan, Northwestern, Chicago, North Carolina, Ohio State, Berkeley, UCLA Tennessee, and many other campuses.

In 1970, in what may be described as a minor visitation, at least in comparison with the vast upsurges of 1858 and 1905 evangelical awakenings occurred at Asbury College, Anderson Taylor, Spring Arbor, Fort Wayne Bible College, Azusa Pacific Oral Roberts, and Southwestern Baptist Seminary, among others

This history of evangelical awakenings on college campuses as well as the accounts of nationwide spiritual revival, reminds us of a significant strand in the development of higher education in the United States and of a powerful current in the American character. Within the past 20 years higher education has become so dominantly secular that many of us tend to forget about, and perhaps some of us are unaware of, the strength of these Protestant antecedents. From the mid-seventeenth century to the mid-twentieth century, higher education was mainly private and mainly Protestant. The 1950 census showed for the first time that the number of students enrolled in public institutions reached equality with the number enrolled in private ones. In the 20 years following 1950, as enrollments grew from 3 million to 8 million, the growth was primarily in the public sector—reflected in the increased size of state universities and the rapid expansion of public junior colleges—so that now the public sector outnumbers the private by a factor of nearly 3 to 1. Moreover, since the private sector includes Catholic colleges and nonsectarian colleges as well as Protestant colleges, the proportionate share of total student enrollment that can be claimed by Protestant colleges today is approximately one-tenth. Yet the power of a heritage or of a special character is often greater than sheer numbers lead one to suppose. This is all the more likely to be true when the special character of the institution is linked to pervasive elements in the larger society or culture—as to religion in the case of denominational colleges, or to technology in the case of specialized schools of engineering and the sciences such as the California and Massachusetts Institutes of Technology.

The church and religious history of America has surely revealed periods of great strength and influence and periods of widespread disinterest and disengagement. The campus picture today is not clear, at least not to this writer. Evangelism is still active but not highly visible. In fact, the fastest-growing segments in Christianity are the Pentecostals—with Pentecostal groups found even on Catholic campuses. Moreover, the establishment of new liberal arts colleges is taking place mainly under the sponsorship of evangelical Christians.

As we examine this campus picture we shall pay special attention to comparisons between the more evangelical-fundamentalist Christian colleges, on the one hand, and the colleges affiliated with the larger and generally more modernist Protestant denominations on the other. Is there a unique Protestant college environment? Do the graduates have attitudes and interests different from those of other colleges and universities? Are the students different from other students? These are the questions to which the next three chapters are addressed.

3. The Environment

If you want to know what it is like in Paducah, Kentucky, ask the people who live there. That is the simple principle behind the reports presented in this chapter. There are many ways of describing a place. One can talk about its physical characteristics— its size and density, whether it is flat or hilly, tropical or temperate, or some other aspect of its setting, such as whether it is rural or urban. One can talk about the people who live there, what sort of work they do, and how they relate to one another. Or one can note the rituals, customs, and beliefs that may be evident. Just as societies can be described by their physical features, their political economy, and their style of life, so colleges can also be described in these ways. Colleges are described by size or residential character; by the sort of admission requirements they have— highly selective or open-door admission, men only, women only, or coeducational; by the programs they offer—liberal arts, engineering, business, etc.; and by other terms that parallel the descriptions of other societies.

The most widely used systematic means for describing college environments is a questionnaire instrument called College and University Environment Scales. Commonly referred to as CUES, this instrument consists of statements about colleges and universities—features and facilities, policies and procedures, curricula, instruction, faculty, student activities and interests—that students mark either "generally true" or "generally not true" in respect to their own campus. Thus, students who live in the college environment serve as reporters about it.

The directions in the test booklet illustrate more precisely what is requested:

Colleges and universities differ from one another in many ways. Some things that are generally true or characteristic of one school may not be characteristic of another. The purpose of the College & University Environment Scales (CUES) is to help describe the general atmosphere of different colleges. The atmosphere of a campus is a mixture of various features, facilities, rules and procedures, faculty characteristics, courses of study, classroom activities, students' interests, extracurricular programs, informal activities, and other conditions and events.

You are asked to be a reporter about your school. You have lived in its environment, seen its features, participated in its activities, and sensed its attitudes. What kind of a place is it?

There are 160 statements in this booklet. You are to answer them True or False, using the answer sheet given you for this purpose.

As you read the statements you will find that many cannot be answered True or False in a literal sense. The statements contain qualifying words or phrases, such as "almost always," "frequently," "generally," and "rarely," and are intended to draw out your impression of whether the situation described applies or does not apply to your campus as you know it.

As a reporter about your college you are to indicate whether you think each statement is generally characteristic, a condition that exists, an event that occurs or might occur, the way people generally act or feel — in short, whether the statement is more nearly True than False; or conversely, whether you think it is not generally characteristic, does not exist or occur, is more nearly False than True.

The CUES is not a test in which there are right or wrong answers; it is more like an opinion poll — a way to find out how much agreement or disagreement there is about the characteristics of a campus environment.

The first edition of CUES was published in 1963 and a second edition in 1969. One hundred statements are common to both editions.[1] Nearly all the reports presented in this chapter are based on Form 1 results that have been rescored to make them comparable to the more recent edition. Most of the reports are based on the use of CUES during the years 1966–1970.

Scores reflect the collective perception of what is characteristic of the campus. If students agree, by a margin of 2 to 1 or greater, that a statement is generally true about their campus, then it is considered to be a "characteristic" of the campus. Characteristic, in this sense, means dominant. Only statements that are answered at this high level of consensus are counted in the score. The score, then, is simply the number of statements that are reported to be "characteristic" of the college.

[1] These statements are listed in Appendix A.

There are five scales or dimensions in the test, each consisting of 20 statements. The scales, labeled Practicality, Community, Awareness, Propriety, and Scholarship, are described below. They reflect major ways in which college environments differ from one another.

- *Practicality* The 20 items that contribute to the score for this scale describe an environment characterized by enterprise, organization, material benefits, and social activities. There are both vocational and collegiate emphases. A kind of orderly supervision is evident in the administration and the classwork. As in many organized societies there is also some personal benefit and prestige to be obtained by operating in the system — knowing the right people, being in the right clubs, becoming a leader, respecting one's superiors, and so forth. The environment, though structured, is not repressive because it responds to entrepreneurial activities and is generally characterized by good fun and school spirit.

- *Community* The items in this scale describe a friendly, cohesive, group-oriented campus. There is a feeling of group welfare and group loyalty that encompasses the college as a whole. The atmosphere is congenial; the campus is a community. Faculty members know the students, are interested in their problems, and go out of their way to be helpful. Student life is characterized by togetherness and sharing rather than by privacy and cool detachment.

- *Awareness* The items in this scale seem to reflect a concern about and emphasis upon three sorts of meaning — personal, poetic, and political. An emphasis upon self-understanding, reflectiveness, and identity suggests the search for personal meaning. A wide range of opportunities for creative and appreciative relationships to painting, music, drama, poetry, sculpture, architecture, and the like suggests the search for poetic meaning. A concern about events around the world, the welfare of mankind, and the present and future condition of man suggests the search for political meaning and idealistic commitment. What seems to be evident in this sort of environment is a stress on awareness, an awareness of self, of society, and of aesthetic stimuli. Along with this push toward expansion, and perhaps as a necessary condition for it, there is an encouragement of questioning and dissent and a tolerance of nonconformity and personal expressiveness.

- *Propriety* These items describe an environment that is polite and considerate. Caution and thoughtfulness are evident. Group standards of decorum are important. There is an absence of demonstrative, assertive, argumentative, risk-taking activities. In general, the campus atmosphere is mannerly, considerate, proper, and conventional.

Scholarship The items in this scale describe an environment characterized by intellectuality and scholastic discipline. The emphasis is on competitively high academic achievement and a serious interest in scholarship. The pursuit of knowledge and theories, scientific or philosophical, is carried on rigorously and vigorously. Intellectual speculation, an interest in ideas, knowledge for its own sake, and intellectual discipline—all these are characteristic of the environment.

One further note is needed to explain the scores. Consensus of 2 to 1 or greater can be in either of two directions—an agreement that the statement is true or an equally high agreement that it is not true. Agreement in the keyed direction is a plus; agreement in the opposite direction is a minus. The score is a combination of plus and minus agreements that reach the level of 2 to 1 or greater. So as to eliminate minus scores, a constant of 20 is added to the algebraic sum. Thus, the scores reported in the following charts range from 0 to 40, with zero meaning that all 20 items were answered by a 2 to 1 consensus in the direction opposite to the scale and 40 meaning that all 20 items were answered by a 2 to 1 consensus in the keyed direction.

During 1965 and 1966, a selected group of 100 colleges and universities was used to constitute a national norm or baseline. These 100 institutions were carefully selected examples of eight types of environments: (1) highly selective liberal arts colleges, private nonsectarian; (2) strongly denominational liberal arts colleges, Protestant and Catholic; (3) other liberal arts colleges, both nonsectarian and denominational; (4) highly selective universities, public and private; (5) general comprehensive universities, public and private; (6) state colleges and other regional or less comprehensive universities, mostly public but some private; (7) colleges and universities having a predominant emphasis on engineering and the sciences; and (8) colleges having a predominant emphasis on teacher training.

The first three categories, all liberal arts colleges, are here combined to form a composite reference group—a group encompassing the variety of liberal arts colleges in the country, Protestant, Catholic, and nonsectarian—specifically 5 Catholic colleges, 15 nonsectarian colleges, and 20 Protestant colleges. Protestant college environments will be compared against this more eclectic set of liberal arts colleges.

The next three categories have also been combined to provide a reference group of universities against which liberal arts colleges, and particularly Protestant liberal arts colleges, may be compared. The university group includes three Catholic universities, three affiliated with Protestant denominations (at least nominally), seven nonsectarian private universities, and twenty-seven state supported universities.

Against the above two reference groups, two groups of Protestant colleges are compared. One consists of 50 colleges identified with what we have chosen to call mainline denominations—Episcopal, Congregational, United Presbyterian, United Methodist, American Baptist, Lutheran, and Disciples. The other consists of 30 colleges affiliated with denominations or interdenominational groups regarded as more fundamentalist or evangelical in emphasis—Brethren, Mennonite, Church of God, Nazarene, Moravian, Free Methodist, Church of Christ, Missouri Synod Lutheran, United States Reformed Presbyterian, Southern Baptist—or other than American Baptist, Quaker, and Interdenominational Evangelical.

MAINLINE DENOMINATIONS

Episcopal

Hobart
Shimer

Congregational

Beloit

Presbyterian

Maryville
Wooster
Blackburn
Lindenwood
Lewis and Clark

Macalester
Waynesburg
Austin
Westminster
Coe
Lafayette
Alma
Hanover
Millikin

Disciples

Atlantic Christian
Lynchburg

Education and evangelism 22

Baptist

Eastern Baptist
Kalamazoo
Ottawa
Keuka
Denison
Franklin
Judson

Methodist

Lambuth
Albion
Tennessee Wesleyan
Columbia College
Western Maryland
Evansville
Illinois Wesleyan
Lycoming
Birmingham Southern

Ohio Northern
University of Puget Sound
Simpson
Allegheny
Cornell College
Randolph Macon Woman's
Philander Smith
Upper Iowa

Lutheran

Luther
Susquehanna
Augustana
Gustavus Adolphus
Carthage
Wittenberg

Quaker*

Earlham

EVANGELICAL OR FUNDAMENTALIST DENOMINATIONS

Brethren

Messiah
Bridgewater
Huntington
Indiana Central
Manchester
Elizabethtown

Mennonite

Eastern Mennonite
Goshen

Bluffton

Church of God

Findlay
Anderson
Warner Pacific

Nazarene

Pasadena

The environment 23

**Presbyterian
(United States Reformed)**

Erskine

Lutheran (Missouri Synod)

Valparaiso
Concordia

**Baptist (other
than American
Baptist)**

Meredith
Stetson
Oaklahoma Baptist

Moravian

Moravian

Free Methodist

Seattle Pacific

Greenville

Church of Christ

Ursinus
Northland

Quaker

Guilford
George Fox
Malone

**Interdenominational
(Evangelical)**

Westmont
Barrington
Gordon

---

* Other Quaker-affiliated colleges are classified elsewhere.

**DIFFERENCES
BETWEEN
MAINLINE AND
EVANGELICAL
COLLEGES**

Scholarship

Figure 1 shows the location of all the institutions on the scholarship scale. Each dot represents one college. Clearly there is a great range of scores among the colleges in each group. Evangelical colleges differ from one another in this respect just as much as universities differ, and just as much as the mainline Protestant colleges differ from one another. The greatest range is reflected in the distribution of scores among the baseline or comparison group of liberal arts colleges.

The horizontal line cuts across the categories of colleges at the median or middle score of the national baseline group of 100 colleges and universities. The two comparison groups shown in

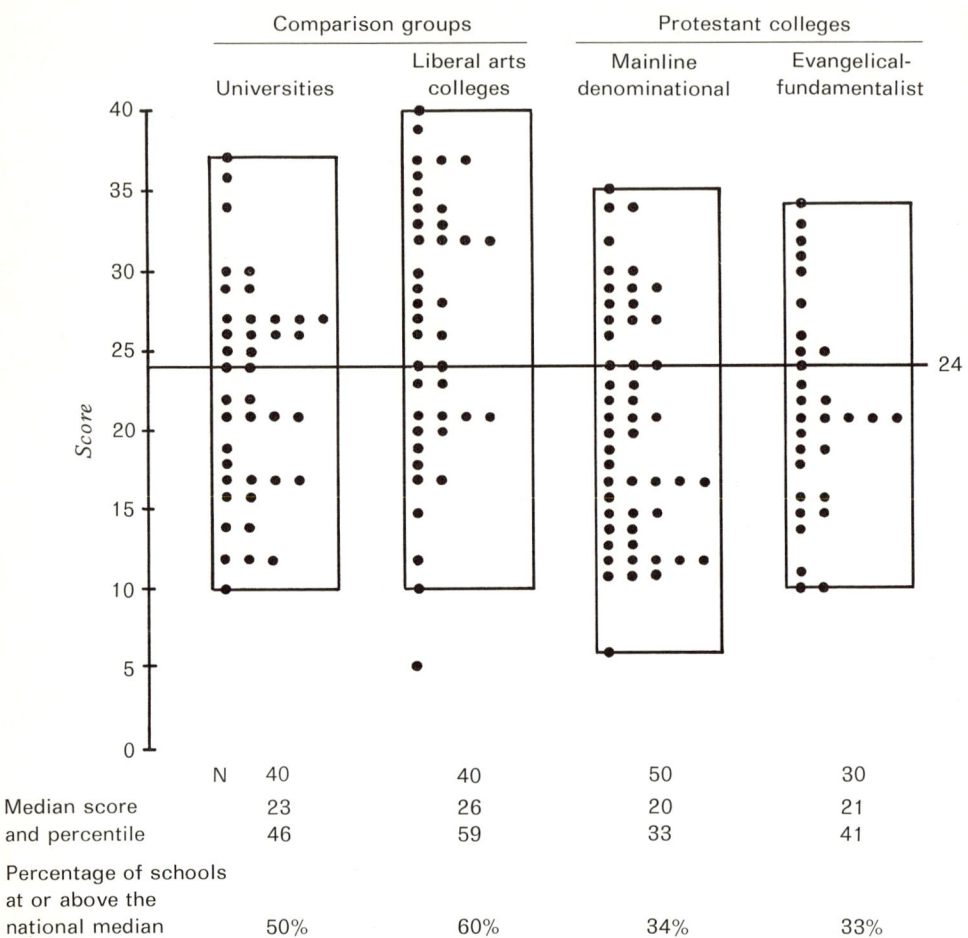

FIGURE 1 *College and university environment scales: SCHOLARSHIP*

the chart comprise 80 of these 100 schools—the remainder being 10 whose primary emphasis is on engineering and sciences and 10 whose primary emphasis is on teacher training. Although in general both mainline and evangelical Protestant colleges are more likely to be below than above the national median, a third of these colleges do score above the median. Obviously, some of them rank with the best in scholarship and others rank with the poorest.

The comparison group of 40 liberal arts colleges includes 16 of the same colleges classified as Protestant colleges. Thus, any differences between the Protestant group and the more inclusive group must be owing mainly to the addition of private nonsectarian institutions to the general comparison group.

In presenting these charts we have enclosed the data in a set of vertical rectangles. Occasionally, however, one or more colleges appear outside the enclosed bars. This is done to highlight the predominant results: whenever a college is left outside the enclosed bar it is because it appears to be a deviant case, an exception to the general distribution. We do not make any special interpretation of this other than to point out that there are exceptions to almost any classification or typology and that they should be seen as exceptions rather than as contradictions to what otherwise is a dominant result.

Awareness

What is most noticeable about the results in Figure 2 is that the evangelical and fundamentalist colleges are more homogeneous than the other groups. None of them has a score higher than 26, which ranks at the 76th percentile on the national baseline. In other words, none of the 30 colleges for which we had data ranked in the top fourth of American colleges and universities. The awareness scale, which reflects emphases on aesthetic and political aspects of the environment, shows results similar to those on the scholarship scale. They indicate that Protestant colleges, whether mainline or evangelical, score generally lower than a more broadly representative (including nonsectarian) set of liberal arts colleges. The main difference between the results on the scholarship and awareness scales is that some evangelical colleges (six of the thirty, or one-fifth) score in the top fourth of colleges nationally on scholarship but none score that high on the awareness scale. Although some mainline Protestant colleges score quite high on the awareness scale, the entire group has the same average as the group of evangelical colleges.

Community

On the community scale, Figure 3, we see a dramatic difference between universities and liberal arts colleges. The catalog cliché about the college being a friendly place—where students know one another well, faculty and students are acquainted with one

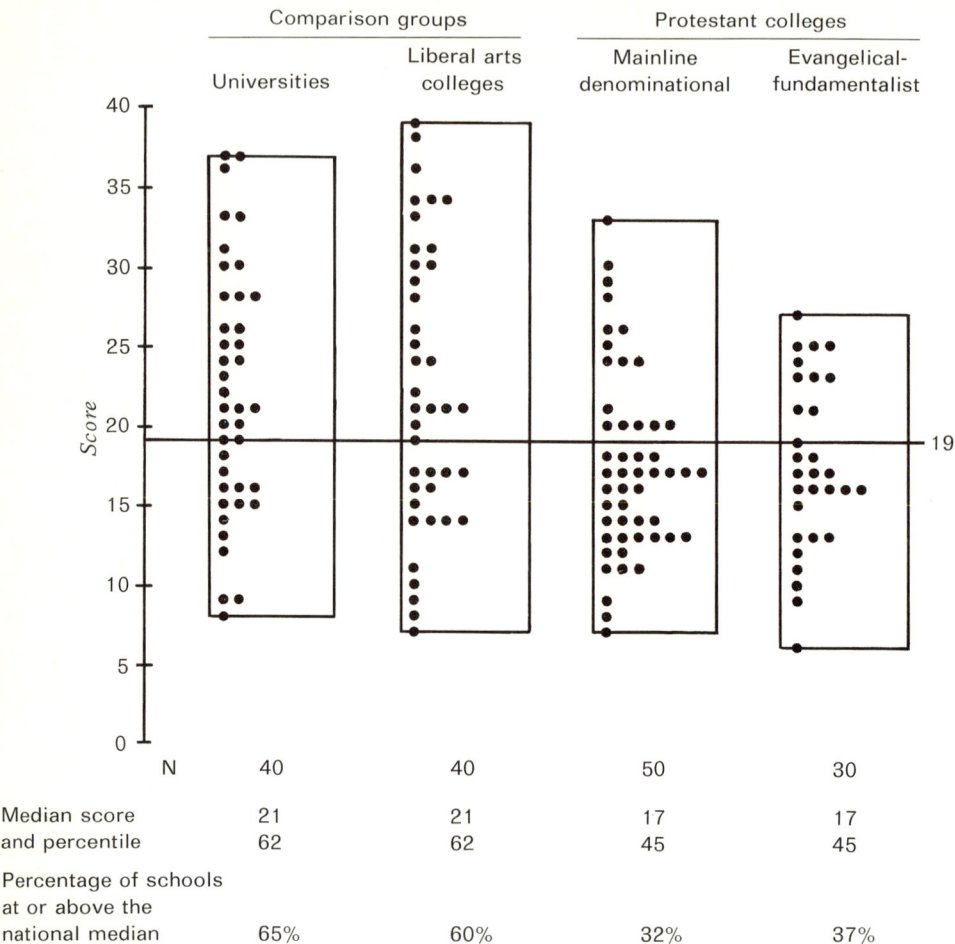

FIGURE 2 *College and university environment scales: AWARENESS*

another, and there is a sense of group welfare and belonging —is really true. Whether the college is mainline Protestant or evangelical Protestant, Catholic or nonsectarian, the liberal arts colleges are perceived by their students as having a sense of community and as being congenial communities. This is not true of the universities, whether highly selective, suburban, and exclusive, such as Princeton or Stanford, or urban and congested, such as Wayne State. Every one of the Protestant colleges, mainline or evangelical, and all but one among the other liberal arts colleges, scored higher than the average of the universities on the community dimension of the environment.

Such a clear contrast is doubtless a function of sheer size, although in some cases it is compounded by a university's urban location. This is not to say that one cannot find a congenial, friendly sense of belonging within a large or urban university. One can. And on every large campus there are opportunities for congenial associations. What is being concluded from the results of CUES is that the sense of community which may well exist within many large universities is not so pervasive that the campus as

FIGURE 3 College and university environment scales: COMMUNITY

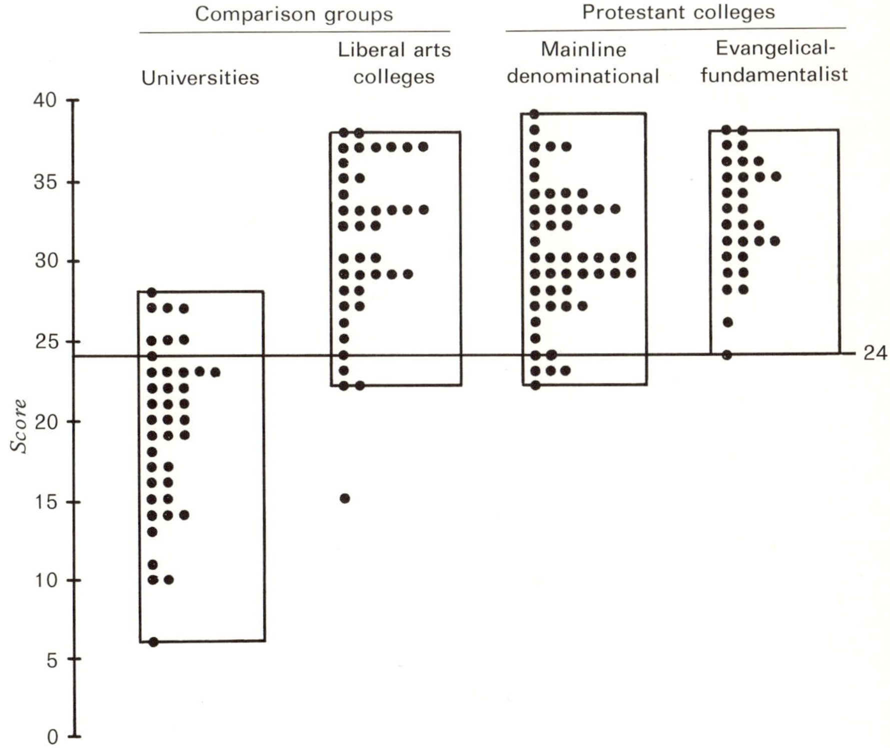

	Comparison groups		Protestant colleges	
	Universities	Liberal arts colleges	Mainline denominational	Evangelical-fundamentalist
N	40	40	50	30
Median score and percentile	20 / 26	32 / 88	30 / 78	32 / 88
Percentage of schools at or above the national median	20%	90%	92%	100%

a whole is perceived to be a warm and congenial community. In the universities, one has to find a neighborhood within the larger city. The liberal arts college is itself a neighborhood.

Propriety

The words *polite, considerate, cautious,* and *thoughtful* are not exactly terms that come to mind in describing the campuses at Stanford, Michigan, Wisconsin, or San Francisco State, or, for that matter, at any college or university where town and gown have clashed and where students are frustrated and outraged by what they believe to be the duplicity, immorality, and lawlessness of the establishment. Such campus feelings would contribute to a low score on the propriety scale, but would probably result in a high score on the awareness scale. The lack of propriety, as measured in CUES, Figure 4, comes more from breaking rules, being spontaneous, engaging in pranks, indulging in rowdy behavior, and being generally contentious and quarrelsome.

Scores for the comparison groups of universities and liberal arts colleges come from data collected in 1965–66. The Berkeley rebellion erupted in November 1964; the student deaths at Jackson State and Kent State and the Cambodian invasion were not until May 1970. The Protestant college scores include some as early as 1965–66 and some as recent as 1969–70. But no data were obtained any later than spring of 1970. Indeed, many colleges had planned to use CUES, second edition, in the spring of 1970. But owing to the impact of Jackson, Kent, and Cambodia, nearly all these plans were postponed.

Even though these data do not reflect the crisis on the campuses, however, most of the universities (70 percent) still scored at or below the national norm (based on 1965–66 testing). Only the evangelical and fundamentalist Protestant colleges remained typically high on the propriety scale, 93 percent of them scoring above the national average. Decorum and a due regard for rules are characteristics of many other liberal arts colleges, too, although some of them, 15 out of 90, scored at a level ranking them in the lowest fourth of the national distribution of scores.

Practicality

In Figure 5, the remarkable similarity among all evangelical-fundamentalist colleges is quite evident. They are all at or above

FIGURE 4 *College and university environment scales: PROPRIETY*

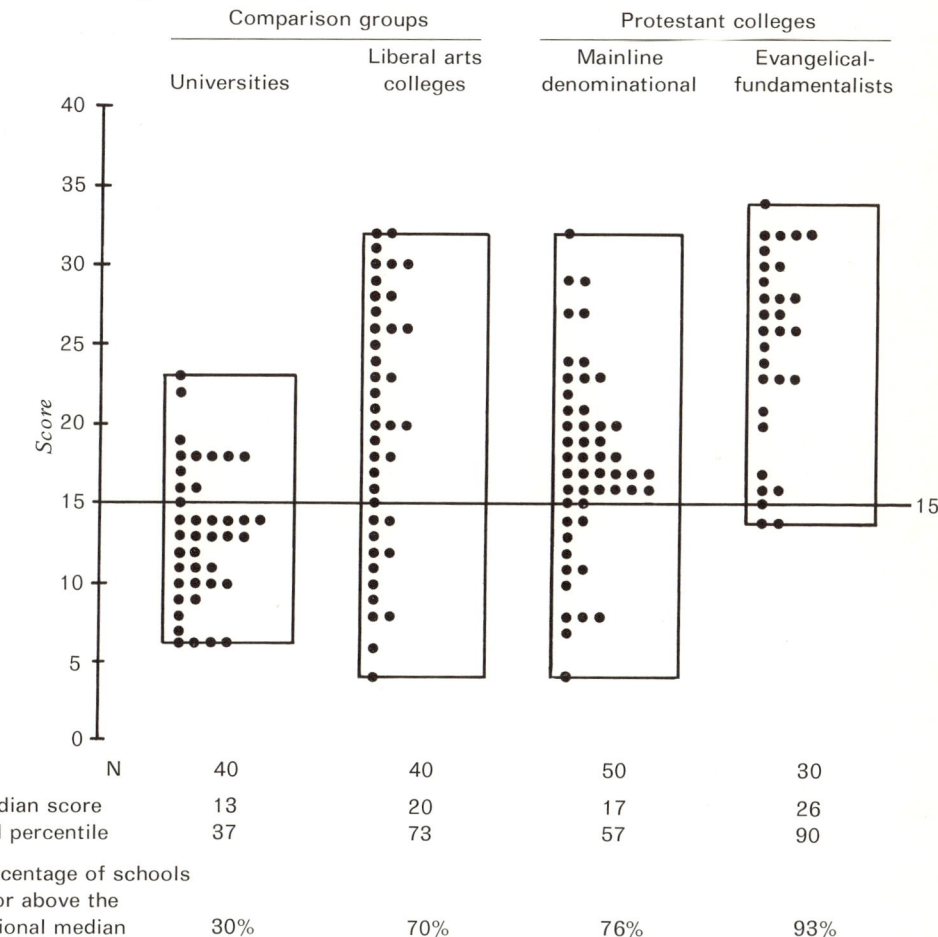

the national average, although none is as far above as some of the schools in each of the other three groups. The greatest degree of consensus among most of these evangelical schools is on the following items:

- The important people at this school expect others to show proper respect for them.
- There is a recognized group of student leaders on the campus.
- Students take a great deal of pride in their personal appearance.
- Frequent tests are given in most courses.

FIGURE 5 *College and university environment scales:* **PRACTICALITY**

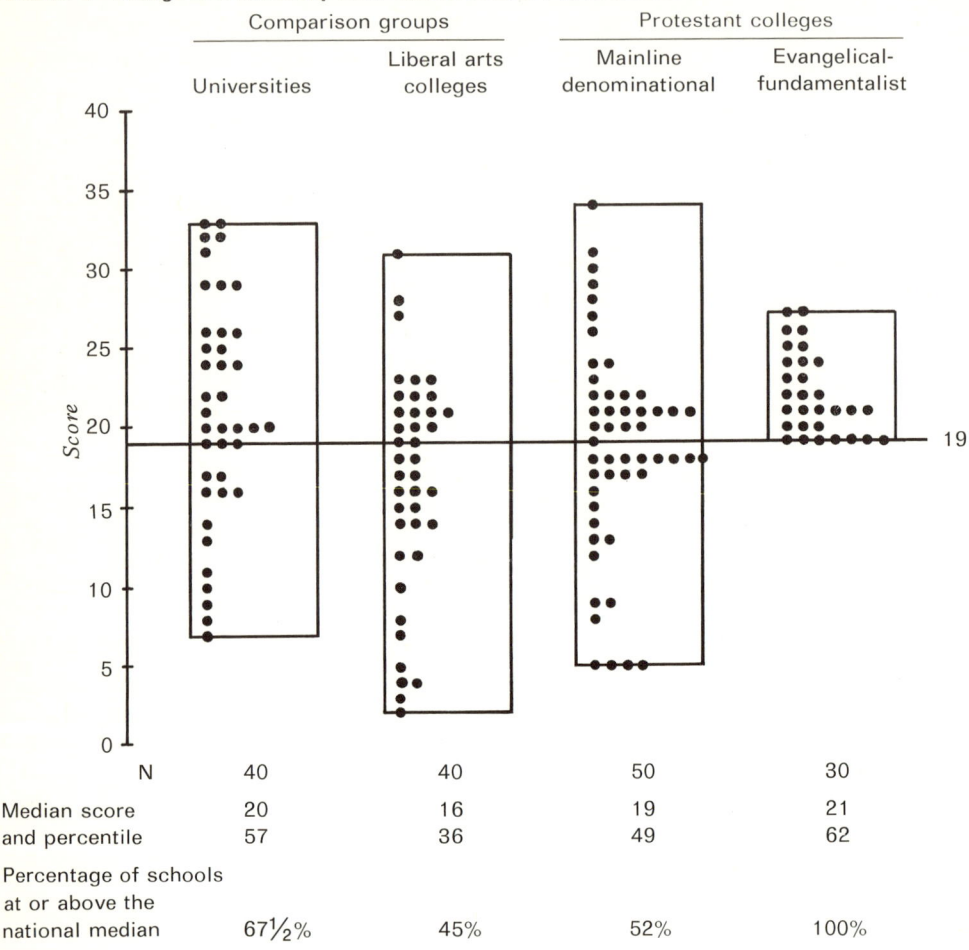

- Big college events draw a lot of student enthusiasm and support.
- Many students try to pattern themselves after people they admire.
- Education here tends to make students more practical and realistic.

Within three of the groups—mainline denominational schools, other liberal arts colleges, and universities—there are large differences among individual institutions. Any one of these colleges or universities might be very high or very low on the practicality scale. There is, however, relatively little difference between any two of these three groups. By contrast, the evangelical-fundamentalist colleges are alike in their concern for leadership and respect and their encouragement of consistent effort toward pragmatic ends.

Is there a Protestant college environment that is in any way distinctive? If all one knew about a liberal arts college was its association with a mainline Protestant denomination, the only thing one could say about it with any assurance is that its general atmosphere will be friendly, supportive, and congenial. Mainline Protestant colleges run the gamut from high to low on the measures of scholarship and awareness, although the average tends to be on the low side. They also run the gamut from high to low on the measures of propriety and practicality, with propriety scores generally on the high side and practicality scores averaging at the middle of the national comparison groups of colleges and universities. The colleges affiliated with evangelical or fundamentalist groups are more distinctive. Not only are they friendly and supportive communities, they are also characterized by almost uniformly high scores on both propriety and practicality. They are undifferentiated from mainline Protestant colleges with regard to scholarship and awareness, a fact indicating that education and evangelism are not incompatible.

Table 1 summarizes the different liberal arts college environments in comparison with the national "norms" for all sorts of colleges and universities. Figure 6 plots the median profiles of each of the groups of universities and colleges we have been describing.

TABLE 1
Summary of different liberal arts college environments

Scales	Percentage of colleges at or above the national median		
	General liberal arts (40 colleges)	Mainline denominational (50 colleges)	Evangelical-fundamentalist (30 colleges)
Scholarship	60	34	33
Awareness	60	32	37
Community	90	90	100
Propriety	70	76	93
Practicality	45	52	100

FIGURE 6 *CUES profiles*

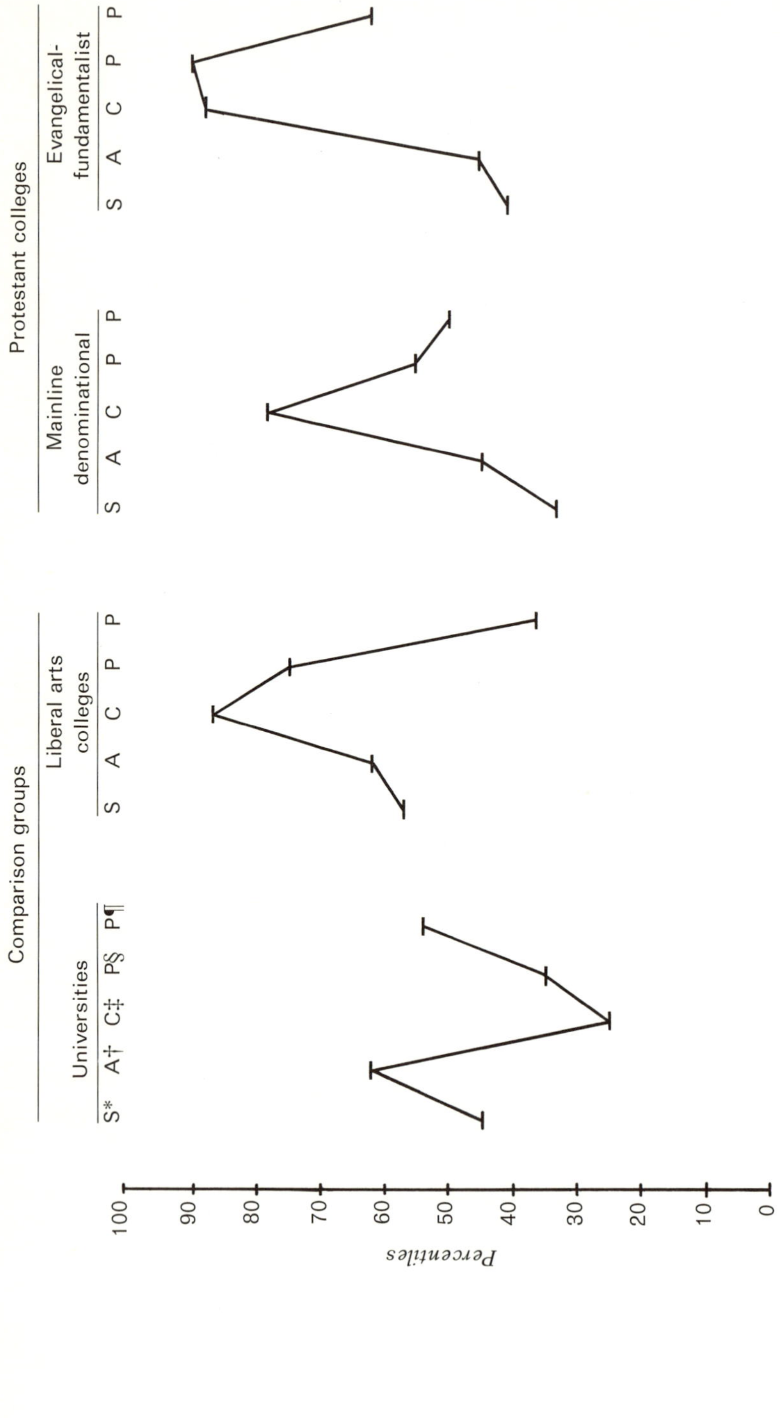

* Scholarship.
† Awareness.
‡ Community.
§ Propriety.
¶ Practicality.

DIFFERENCES RELATED TO STRENGTH OF CHURCH CONNECTIONS

Perhaps even sharper differentiations among Protestant colleges would be revealed if, instead of comparing mainline and evangelical denominations, we classified the colleges according to the nature and extent of their connection with a denomination, whatever that denomination might be. The Danforth Foundation's extensive survey that was reported in 1966 (*Church-Sponsored Higher Education in the United States,* by Pattillo & MacKenzie) identifies six types of denominational connections.

1 Board of control includes members of church and/or members nominated or elected by church body.
2 Ownership of the institution by the religious body.
3 Financial support by the religious body.
4 Acceptance by the institution of denominational standards or use of the denominational name.
5 Institutional statement of purpose linked to a particular denomination or reflecting religious orientation.
6 Church membership a factor in selection of faculty and administrative personnel.

In 1963, administrations of 817 church-sponsored colleges classified their institutions with respect to each of the six relationships. Some of the classifications may be different today, but no more recent survey has been made. We have therefore taken the classifications reported in the Pattillo and MacKenzie study for each of the 80 Protestant colleges for which we have reported CUES scores and have grouped them to reflect different degrees of control:

Group 1 Colleges reporting *all six* of the relationships noted above: Eastern Mennonite, Messiah, George Fox, Bridgewater, Goshen, Augustana, Lambuth, Columbia (Methodist), Anderson, Huntington, Lewis and Clark, Austin, Ohio Northern, Meredith, Concordia, Erskine, and Pasadena. To this group we have arbitrarily added three interdenominational yet strongly Protestant and evangelical institutions: Westmont, Barrington, and Gordon.

Group 2 Colleges reporting *all of the first three* relationships. These involve trustees, ownership, and money. Any one or two of the remaining relationships, but not all three, may also have been claimed. These colleges are Tennessee Wesleyan, Elizabethtown, Manchester, Oklahoma Baptist, Lycoming, Wittenberg, Westminster, Gustavus Adolphus, Valparaiso, Carthage, Judson, Warner Pacific, Birmingham Southern, and Malone.

Group 3 This group includes colleges that identified all types of connection except ownership by the denomination. They include Luther, Maryville, Seattle Pacific, Wooster, Susquehanna, Eastern Baptist, Greenville, Kalamazoo, Stetson, Indiana Central, Bluffton, Illinois Wesleyan, Lynchburg, Waynesburg, Hanover, Millikin, and Moravian.

Group 4 This group includes institutions acknowledging a connection with the board of trustees and financial support from the denomination; or, having one of these two types of connection, plus some other connections, but not including ownership. The colleges are Blackburn, Atlantic Christian, Earlham, Western Maryland, Denison, Franklin, University of Puget Sound, Simpson, Allegheny, Alma, Findlay, Guilford, Ottawa, Evansville, Cornell, and Hobart.

Group 5 The final group includes colleges having no official connections with a denomination through the composition of the board of trustees and colleges not owned by the denomination. They may have any of the remaining types of connections. These colleges are Albion, Lindenwood, Beloit, Macalester, Keuka, Shimer, Coe, Lafayette, Randolph Macon Woman's College, Ursinus, Philander Smith, Northland, and the University of Tulsa.

The first two groups involve legal ownership *and* trustee influence in governance *and* financial support from the denomination. These are the strongest legal connections. The only difference between the first and second group is in the number of other connections that are claimed. In the first group all six kinds of relationship are operative.

The middle group, or Group 3, includes many institutions with strong denominational ties. But one crucial tie is missing: the denomination does not legally own the college. All the other types of relationship, however, are present.

The difference between Groups 4 and 5 is the presence of denominational representation on the governing board. Group

4 colleges have such representation; Group 5 colleges do not. In neither group, of course, does the denomination own the college.

The environmental differences that are revealed when Protestant colleges are grouped in these ways are depicted in the next five charts. With respect to the scholarship scores, Figure 7, the nature and strength of denominational control or influence seems to make little difference. What accounts for the split among colleges in Group 3 is not known. This peculiarity gives to Group 3 schools a lower *median* score than they deserve. The *mean* of the group is 21, which is also the median of the other groups. A similar split among colleges in Group 5 occurs in Figure 8, which

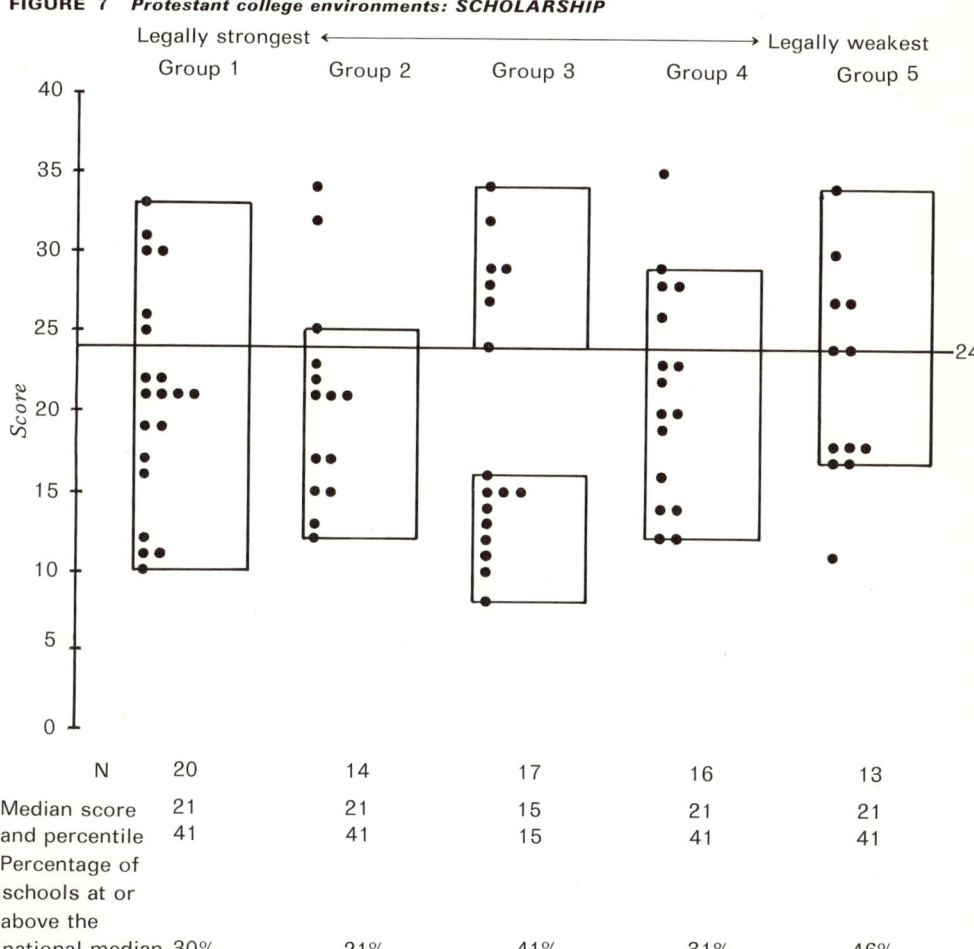

FIGURE 7 *Protestant college environments: SCHOLARSHIP*

FIGURE 8 ***Protestant college environments: AWARENESS***

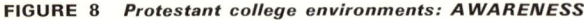

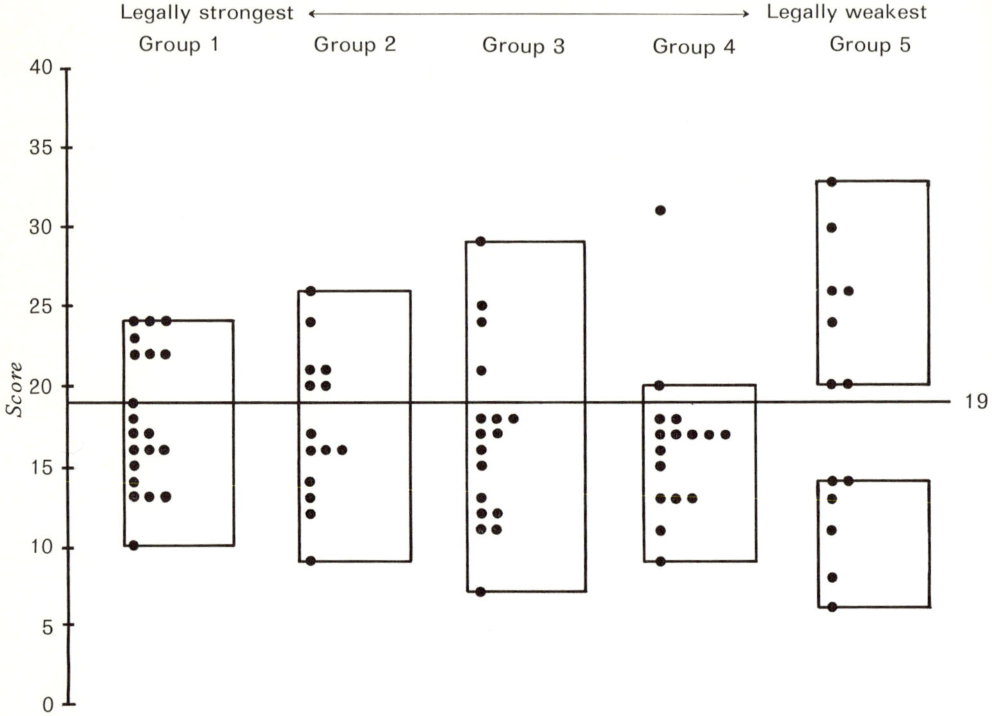

	Group 1	Group 2	Group 3	Group 4	Group 5
N	20	14	17	16	13
Median score	17	16	17	17	20
and percentile	45	39	45	45	55
Percentage of schools at or above the national median	40%	43%	24%	12½%	54%

shows the awareness scores. All the colleges in the upper group are identified with mainline denominations. In Figure 7, however, three of the seven colleges in the upper scholarship group were identified with evangelical or fundamentalist denominations. On the community scale, Figure 9, owing to the consistency of the results, it seems fair to say that the stronger the legal and spiritual ties, the greater the sense of community. This same consistent direction is also clear on the propriety and practicality scales, Figures 10 and 11.

Table 2 summarizes these trends in a manner similar to the summarization in Table 1. Whether one sorts the colleges into

FIGURE 9 *Protestant college environments: COMMUNITY*

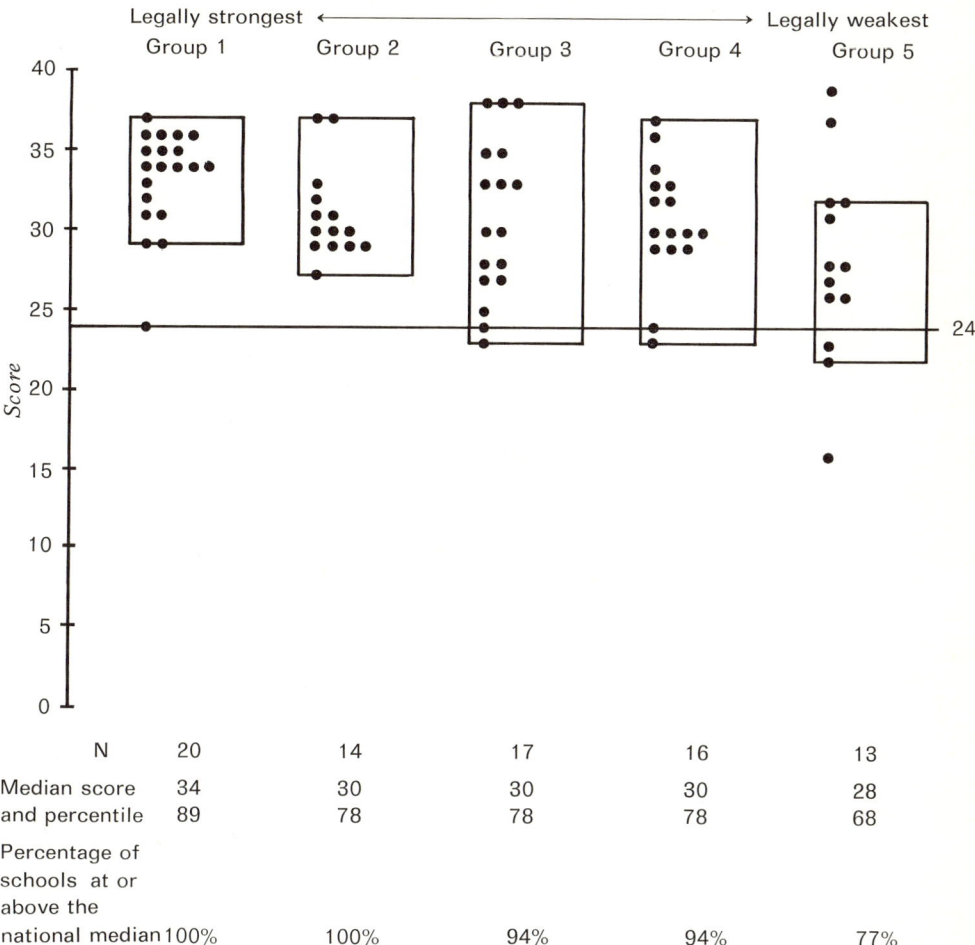

mainline versus evangelical-fundamentalist groups or classifies them along some index of closeness of association with a denomination, regardless of which denomination, one finds that the more firmly and zealously a college is related to a church the more clearly it emerges as a distinctive college environment. And this distinctiveness is defined by uniformly high scores on the characteristics labeled community, propriety, and practicality. Moreover, on all five measures, the environments of mainline denominational colleges show a greater diversity or range of difference than those of the evangelical-fundamentalist colleges. With respect to most of these dimensions, the colleges most loosely connected with the

FIGURE 10 *Protestant college environments: PROPRIETY*

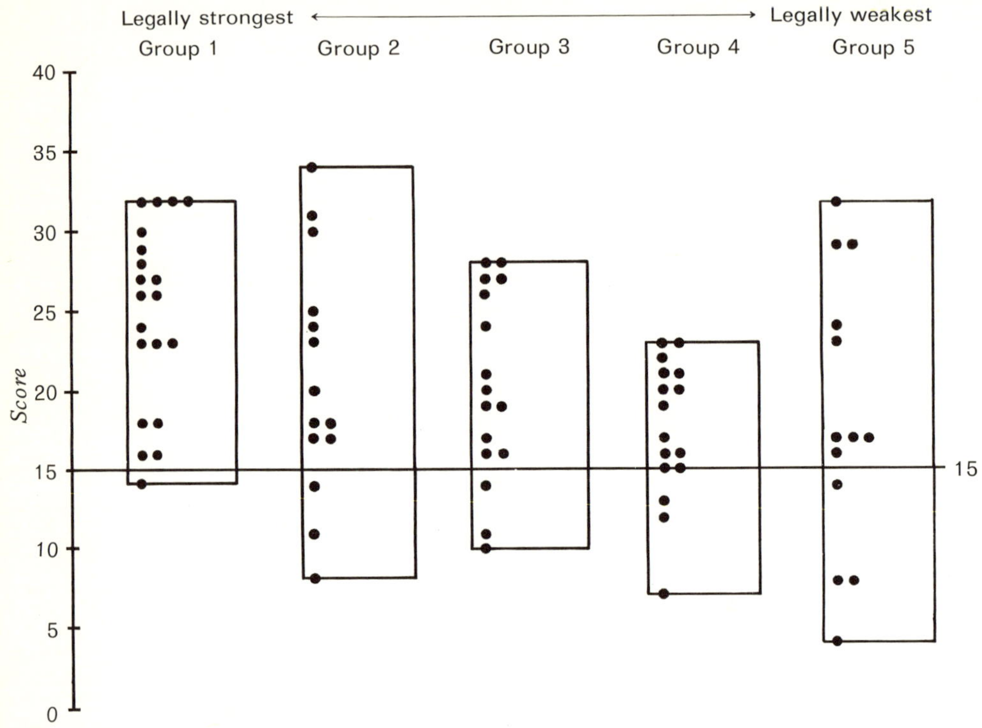

Legally strongest ←――――――――――――――――――→ Legally weakest

	Group 1	Group 2	Group 3	Group 4	Group 5
N	20	14	17	16	13
Median score and percentile	26 / 90	19 / 69	19 / 69	18 / 65	17 / 57
Percentage of schools at or above the national median	95%	79%	82%	81%	60%

church are also more diverse, or less homogeneous, than ones closely tied to the church.

A DIAGNOSTIC LOOK AT SPECIFIC CHARACTERISTICS

The scales for scholarship and awareness are quite similar for all denominational groups, yet on both scales there seemed to be potential differences that were not being revealed. There was, for example, an indication that the most loosely affiliated denominational colleges had somewhat higher scholarship and awareness scores than the others; and the average scores for the comparison group of 40 colleges (which included many nonsec-

The environment 39

FIGURE 11 *Protestant college environments: PRACTICALITY*

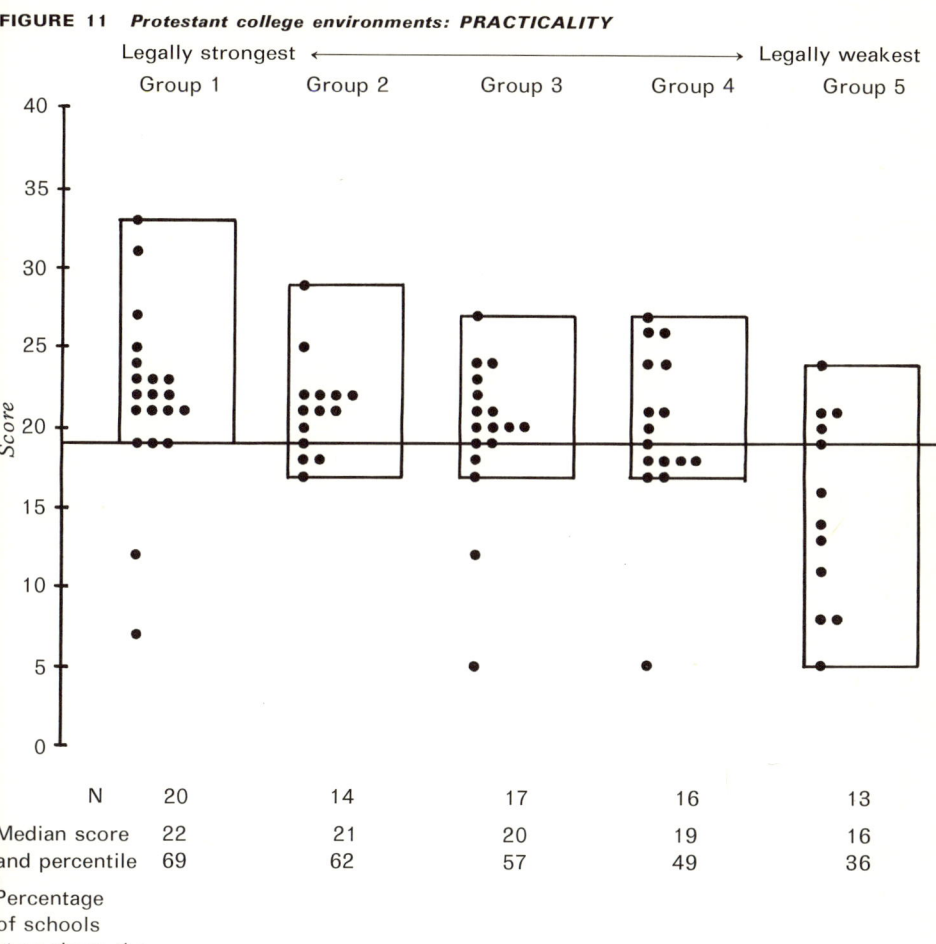

	Group 1	Group 2	Group 3	Group 4	Group 5
N	20	14	17	16	13
Median score and percentile	22 69	21 62	20 57	19 49	16 36
Percentage of schools at or above the national median	90%	79%	76%	56%	46%

TABLE 2 *Summary of protestant college environments in relation to strength of association with the church*

	Percentage of colleges at or above the national median				
Scales	Strongly connected Group 1	Group 2	Group 3	Group 4	Loosely connected Group 5
Scholarship	30	21	41	31	46
Awareness	40	43	24	12½	54
Community	100	100	94	94	77
Propriety	95	79	82	81	60
Practicality	90	79	76	56	46

tarian ones) were higher than those for either group of denominational colleges.

To look more closely, and perhaps more diagnostically, at the data, we took four rather loosely connected colleges out of the mainline denominational group of fifty colleges, added four others that had some Protestant heritage but were not listed in the Danforth Report, and thereby formed a small set of eight colleges that we call Protestant-independent. The colleges are Earlham, Shimer, Hobart, and Beloit, plus Colgate, Colby, Rollins, and William Smith.

At this point, instead of looking at scores we looked specifically at all 20 items in each of the five scales, trying to discover more explicit patterns, or trends, or characteristics within or among these three groupings of colleges: (1) Protestant-independent, (2) Mainline denominational, and (3) Evangelical-fundamentalist. The following tabulation illustrates, for one item, the type of information we examined for all items:

Item: Student organizations are closely supervised to guard against mistakes.
Keyed response: True

Percentage of students answering in the keyed direction	Protestant-independent colleges	Mainline denominational colleges	Evangelical-fundamentalist colleges
90–99			
80–89			
70–79		3	3
60–69		8	5
50–59		8	13
40–49	1	8	4
30–39	2	8	4
20–29	2	5	1
10–19	2	5	
0–9	1	1	
Number of colleges	8	46	30
Median percentage	25	45	55

Across the set of 30 evangelical-fundamentalist colleges approximately 55 percent of the students said it was true of their campus that "student organizations are closely supervised to guard against mistakes." At the other two types of schools the corresponding percentages were 45 percent and 25 percent. The trend here is from the highest percentage at the evangelical-fundamentalist schools to the lowest percentage at the independent schools. This is the first of the four possible patterns shown below. The second pattern is simply a straight trend in the opposite direction. In the third and fourth patterns the mainline denominational schools are either the highest or the lowest of the three groups.

Pattern 1
- *Highest* — Evangelical-fundamentalist
- *Middle* — Mainline denominational
- *Lowest* — Protestant-independent

Pattern 2
- *Highest* — Protestant-independent
- *Middle* — Mainline denominational
- *Lowest* — Evangelical-fundamentalist

Pattern 3
- *Highest* — Mainline denominational
- *Lower* — Protestant-independent   Evangelical-fundamentalist

Pattern 4
- *Higher* — Protestant-independent   Evangelical-fundamentalist
- *Lowest* — Mainline denominational

For 18 of the 20 items in the propriety scale the trend line is identical. The highest percentage in the direction of propriety is found in the evangelical-fundamentalist group of colleges. Moreover, the differences between this highest group and one or both of the other groups are substantial.

On the community scale this same pattern is also dominant, with 13 of the 20 items following this straightline trend. Only one item has the opposite pattern; four have the pattern in which the mainline denominational schools are highest, and for two items the mainline schools are lowest. In all of these less dominant patterns, however, there is less than a 10 percent difference between the highest and lowest percentages. For the dominant pattern, 11 of the 13 items have a difference of greater than 10 percent among the groups.

Pattern 1 is also dominant for the practicality scale items, 11 of the 20 following this straightline trend and all 11 showing differences of more than 10 percent among the groups. There is, however, a strong secondary trend for Pattern 3, with the highest percentages reported from the mainline denominational colleges. Six items follow this pattern and four of the six have differences among groups of greater than 10 percent. To account for the remaining three of the items, one was in Pattern 4 and two were ties and so were not counted as being in any pattern.

The percentages were highest for the colleges related to mainline Protestant denominations on the following six items:

	PI	M	EF
Students must have a written excuse for absence from class.	10	63	62
New fads and phrases are continually springing up among the students.	50	52	48
It's important socially here to be in the right club or group.	35	57	25
Student rooms are more likely to be decorated with pennants and pin-ups than with paintings, carvings, mobiles, fabrics, etc.	30	56	50
Anyone who knows the right people in the faculty or administration can get a better break here.	45	52	43
Students almost always wait to be called on before speaking in class.	47	57	54

In both the awareness and the scholarship scales there are a number of items in which the position of the mainline colleges is reversed—i.e., lowest instead of highest.

Although in the dominant pattern of responses for the awareness scale the highest percentages are from the Protestant-independent group of colleges (11 of the 20 items, and with differences of 10 percent or more in 6 of the 11), there is also a strong secondary pattern in which the mainline schools have the lowest percentages on 6 of the 20 items, 5 of the 6 having differences of greater than 10 percent. These items are as follows:

	PI	M	EF
Channels for expressing students' complaints are readily accessible.	70	59	67
There would be a capacity audience for a lecture by an outstanding philosopher or theologian.	50	29	40
The expression of strong personal belief or conviction is pretty rare around here. (Not True)	70	62	83
Concerts and art exhibits always draw big crowds of students.	30	19	25
There is considerable interest in the analysis of value systems, and the relativity of societies and ethics.	60	51	62
Students are encouraged to take an active part in social reforms or political programs.	47	42	46

For items in the scholarship scale the dominant pattern is for the lowest percentages to come from the mainline Protestant colleges. Ten of the 20 items are in this pattern. For 7 of the 20 items the evangelical-fundamentalist colleges have the highest percentages; and for 3 of the 20 items the Protestant-independent colleges were highest. One characteristic of the responses to the scholarship items is that the differences among the three college groups are very small—on 14 of the 20 items the difference between the highest and lowest percentages is less than 10 points. The significance of the results rests more on the substance of the differences than on their magnitude. Items from the scholarship scale on which the lowest percentages come from the mainline colleges are as follows:

	PI	M	EF
The professors really push the students' capacities to the limit.	26	25	48
Class discussions are typically vigorous and intense.	30	23	27
Personality, pull, and bluff get students through many courses. (Not True)	63	58	65

	PI	M	EF
Standards set by the professors are not particularly hard to achieve. (Not True)	60	46	51
Students put a lot of energy into everything they do in class and out.	30	28	35
There is a lot of interest in the philosophy and methods of science.	40	35	40
Most courses require intensive study and preparation out of class.	73	65	68
Most courses are a real intellectual challenge.	43	39	44
People around here seem to thrive on difficulty—the tougher things get the harder they work.	43	40	45
There is very little studying here over the weekends. (Not True)	55	47	54

Looking back at the three sets of items for which the mainline Protestant colleges had either the highest or the lowest percentages, one can piece together a picture of low energy, low exposure, and low involvement. Many of the items have to do with the amount of energy devoted to academic and intellectual pursuits—faculty demands, class discussions, preparations and study effort, and intellectual challenge. Relative lack of interest in and encounter with such matters as philosophy of science, theology, value systems, and the arts suggest a low-exposure environment. Items about expression of complaints and personal convictions and about activity related to social reforms or political programs suggest a low-involvement, low-commitment atmosphere. Energies that might be devoted to these ideas, issues, and activities seem rather to be devoted to new fads and phrases, pennants and pinups, bluff, getting into the right clubs, and knowing the right people.

Lacking strong commitments to the church and to spiritual experience, as well as to scholarship and the world of ideas, some of these Protestant colleges emerge from our array of data as tepid environments. Neither warmly spiritual nor coolly intellectual, they are essentially without vigor and sooner or later, perhaps, will become nonviable.

On a more positive note, we end this chapter by reminding the reader that what we have described as tepid environments are the exception, not the rule, among Protestant colleges. If we take a rather rigorous definition of such an environment as one that ranks within the lowest third of colleges and universities on both scholarship and awareness and within the highest third on the practicality dimension of CUES, we find that 7 of the 50 mainline denominational schools fit our definition.

4. The Graduates

During the first few months of 1969, about 15,000 questionnaires were mailed to samples of college graduates, class of 1950, from 74 different colleges and universities (*Alumni Survey,* 1969). This undertaking was one part of a national evaluation of higher education that had been planned and is being carried out under the direction of the author. Parallel questionnaires were also administered during the calendar year 1969 to samples of incoming freshmen and to upperclassmen. In all, 88 colleges and universities cooperated in these surveys, 59 participating in all three and the others engaging in one or two. Further information about the participating institutions was obtained from directories, catalogs, and other sources. Major analyses of these nationwide surveys are in progress. What appears here and in the following chapter are explorations of the data obtained from Protestant colleges and some comparisons with composite results from the national baseline colleges and universities.

The 74 colleges and universities in the alumni study include examples of all eight types of institutions noted in the previous chapter. From the larger institutions names and addresses of 300 graduates were requested; and from the smaller institutions 150 were requested. Of course, not all the addresses were correct, not everyone answered the questionnaires, and not all the ones returned were usable. Our national baseline or comparison group (with minor exceptions) consists of about 8,300 men and women who received a bachelor's degree in June 1950. This represents a return from about 60 percent of those who received the questionnaire.

The graduates of Protestant colleges, the prime subjects of this chapter, come from 19 colleges. As in some of our previous analyses we have grouped the colleges into three categories.

Protestant-independent

Beloit (Congregational, Presbyterian)
Earlham (Quaker)
Colgate (Private independent, with some Protestant history)

Evangelical-fundamentalist

Concordia (Missouri Synod Lutheran)
Bridgewater (Brethren)
Goshen (Mennonite)
Pepperdine (Church of Christ)
Westmont (Interdenominational)

Mainline denominational

Blackburn (Presbyterian)
Lewis and Clark (Presbyterian)
Macalester (Presbyterian)
Monmouth (Presbyterian)
Albion (Methodist)
Drew (Methodist)
Lycoming (Methodist)
Denison (Baptist)
Redlands (Baptist)
Susquehanna (Lutheran)
Wittenberg (Lutheran)

The college graduates of midcentury, by the time they graduated from college, had experienced two events that are deeply etched in the nation's twentieth century consciousness—the depression years of the 1930s and the war years of the 1940s. The class of 1950 also included a disproportionately large number of men. Many who had been away in the armed forces had returned to college under the GI Bill. Nearly 20 years later, when our questionnaire survey was made, they were mostly in the age group of 40 to 45, with children of their own coming of college age. The class of 1950 had grown up in small towns or in cities that had not yet reached metropolitan dimensions; today a majority of them live in towns and cities with populations of less than 500,000. Most of them (63 percent) identify themselves as Protestants; as Republicans (54 percent); and as professionals or executives (88 percent of the men). Sixty-two percent report family incomes of more than $15,000. Alumni from the 19 Protestant colleges (the 19 are included among the 74) are, as one would expect, much more likely to be Protestants—82 percent of them are and 93 percent of their parents are. Their activities and interests, attitudes and values, and views about education are described in the next several sections of this chapter.

ESTIMATES OF EDUCATIONAL BENEFITS

One section of the questionnaire began as follows: "In thinking back to your undergraduate experience in college or university to what extent do you feel that you were influenced or benefited in each of the following respects?" To each of the 17 statements listed below, one could respond by checking "very much," "quite a bit," "some," or "very little." The statements are in the order in which they appeared in the questionnaire.

Vocational training—skills and techniques directly applicable to a job.

Background and specialization for further education in some professional, scientific or scholarly field.

Broadened literary acquaintance and appreciation.

Awareness of different philosophies, cultures, and ways of life.

Social development—experience and skill in relating to other people.

Personal development—understanding one's abilities and limitations, interests, and standards of behavior.

Critical thinking—logic, inference, nature and limitations of knowledge.

Aesthetic sensitivity—appreciation and enjoyment of art, music, drama.

Writing and speaking—clear, correct, effective communication.

Science and technology—understanding and appreciation.

Citizenship—understanding and interest in the style and quality of civic and political life.

Appreciation of individuality and independence of thought and action.

Development of friendships and loyalties of lasting value.

Vocabulary, terminology, and facts in various fields of knowledge.

Appreciation of religion—moral and ethical standards.

Tolerance and understanding of other people and their values.

Bases for improved social and economic status.

In Table 3 the statements are abbreviated and rearranged in high to low order based on the percentage of alumni who marked them "very much" or "quite a bit." The corresponding percentages from each of the three groupings of Protestant colleges are also shown. The benefit most commonly noted by the total group, "vocabulary, terminology, and facts in various fields of knowl-

TABLE 3
Educational benefits: relative attainment of different groups of alumni

Benefits with respect to:	Percentage of alumni indicating that they were benefited or influenced "very much" or "quite a bit"			
	National baseline	Protestant Colleges		
		Independent	Mainline	Evangelical
Vocabulary	79	78	78	76
Critical thinking	73	78	70	66
Personal development	66	68	69	70
Specialization	65	52	62	69
Philosophy, cultures	64	79	70	68
Social, economic status	64	64	65	60
Communication	63	68	65	66
Literature	62	74	71	72
Social development	62	72	71	70
Individuality	61	72	68	61
Tolerance	57	64	67	73
Science	55	44	45	36
Friendships	54	53	58	70
Art, music, drama	44	59	57	60
Vocational training	43	27	32	47
Citizenship	37	46	46	40
Religion	31	39	48	74

edge," was also noted by almost exactly the same percentage of alumni from each group of Protestant colleges. In contrast, the benefit least commonly noted by the total group, "appreciation of religion—moral and ethical standards," is marked quite differently by the various Protestant groups.

The particular ways in which the Protestant colleges differ from the national group of colleges and universities are more clearly shown in the next three charts.

In Figure 12 the alumni responses for the three Protestant-independent colleges are compared with the national baseline. The stepwise line running across the chart shows the national baseline data (the same percentages as reported in Table 3). The deviations from this baseline are then portrayed by the lines that run above and below it. There are, for example, three lines that extend for a considerable distance below the baseline or comparison group. Alumni of these Protestant-independent colleges are much less likely than alumni in general to claim benefits related to specialization, science, and vocational training. On the other hand, they are much more likely to have felt benefited or influenced with respect to the objectives related to philosophies and cultures, literature, social development, individuality and independence, tolerance, the arts, citizenship, and religion.

The results from graduates of the 11 mainline denominational schools, shown in Figure 13, are quite parallel to the results for the Protestant-independent schools. They are noticeably above the national baseline on exactly the same eight objectives; and they are noticeably below on two of the same three—science and vocational training. They are not significantly below on the benefit related to specialization.

The college benefits claimed by alumni of the 5 evangelical-fundamentalist colleges, Figure 14, are nearly identical (within 5 percentage points) to those claimed by the national group on 9 of the 17 statements. The influence of religion is the most distinctive and strong characteristic of this group's response. There is also a very noticeably above-average influence on the development of friendships and loyalties; and one very noticeably below-average influence related to science. The only other below-average influence of any significance (7 percentage points) relates to the objective of critical thinking.

Is there a special Protestant college influence? The question is too general. We do not have comparisons between Protestant

FIGURE 12 Educational benefits: national baseline versus Protestant-independent self-estimates of progress by alumni

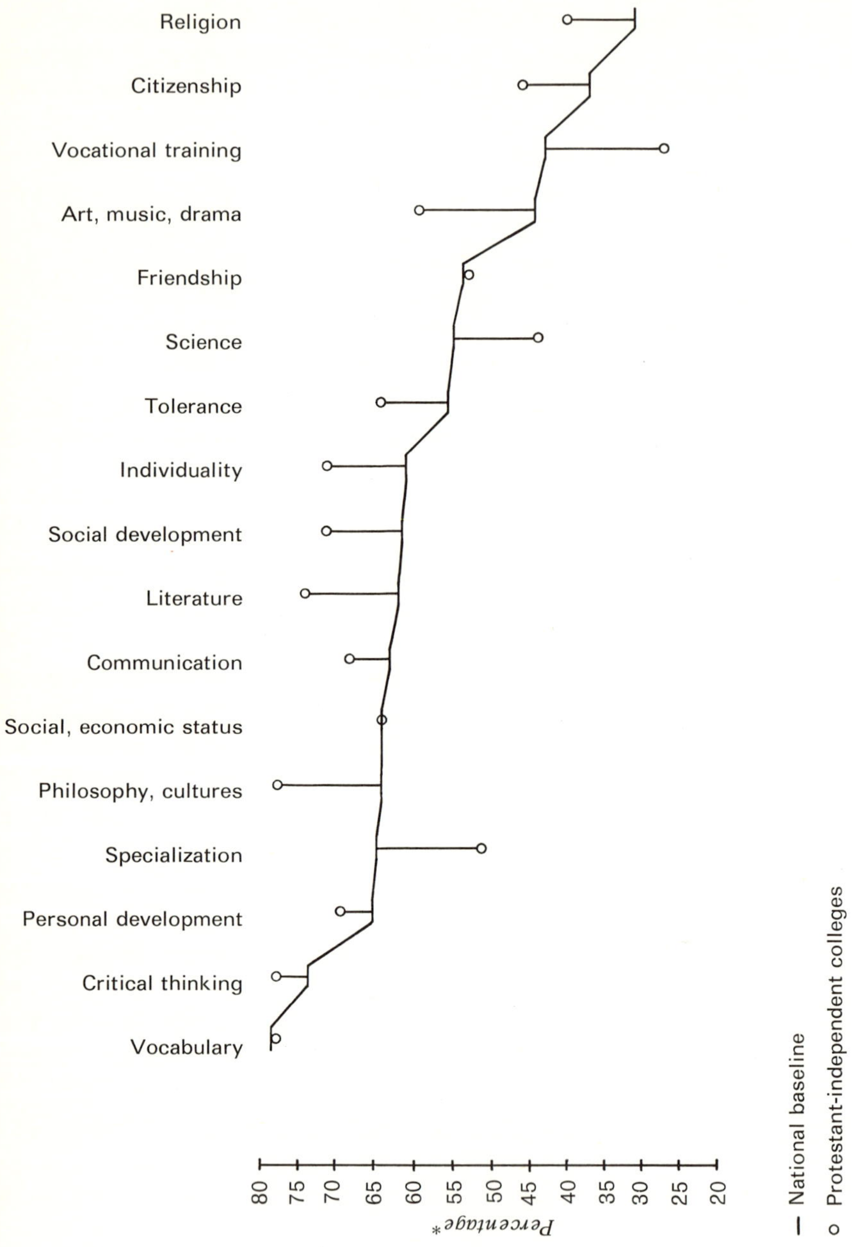

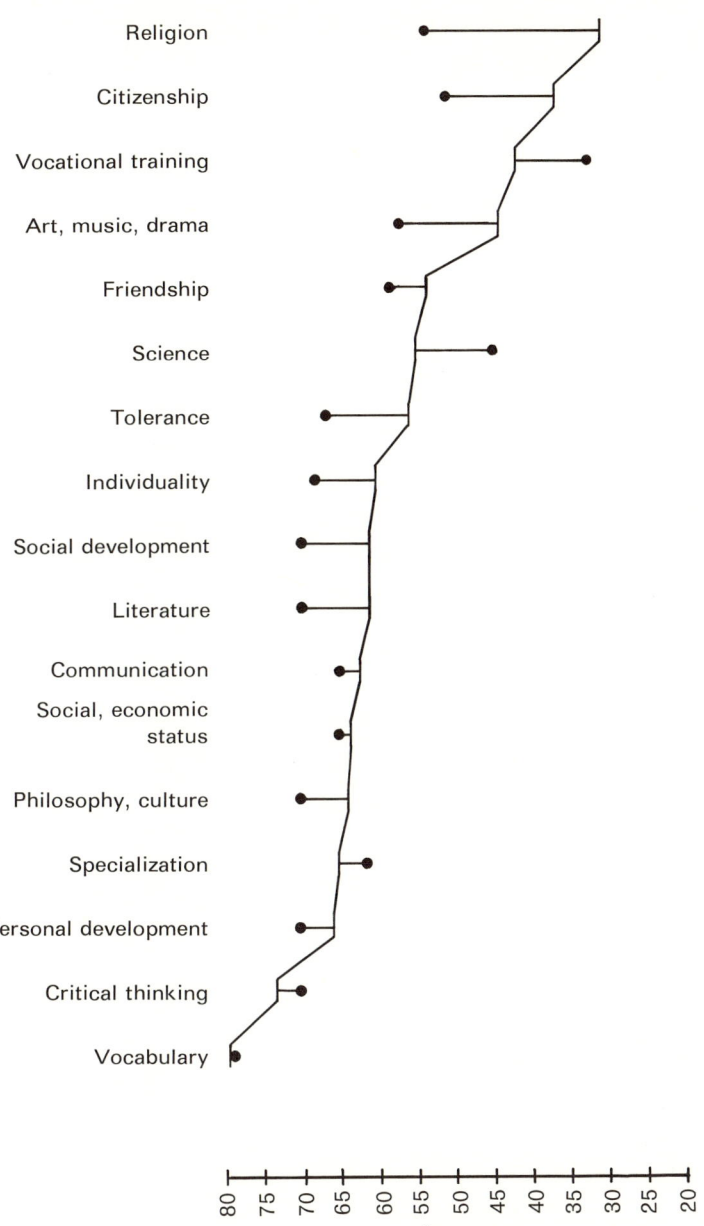

FIGURE 13 *Educational benefits: national baseline versus mainline denominational self-estimates of progress by alumni*

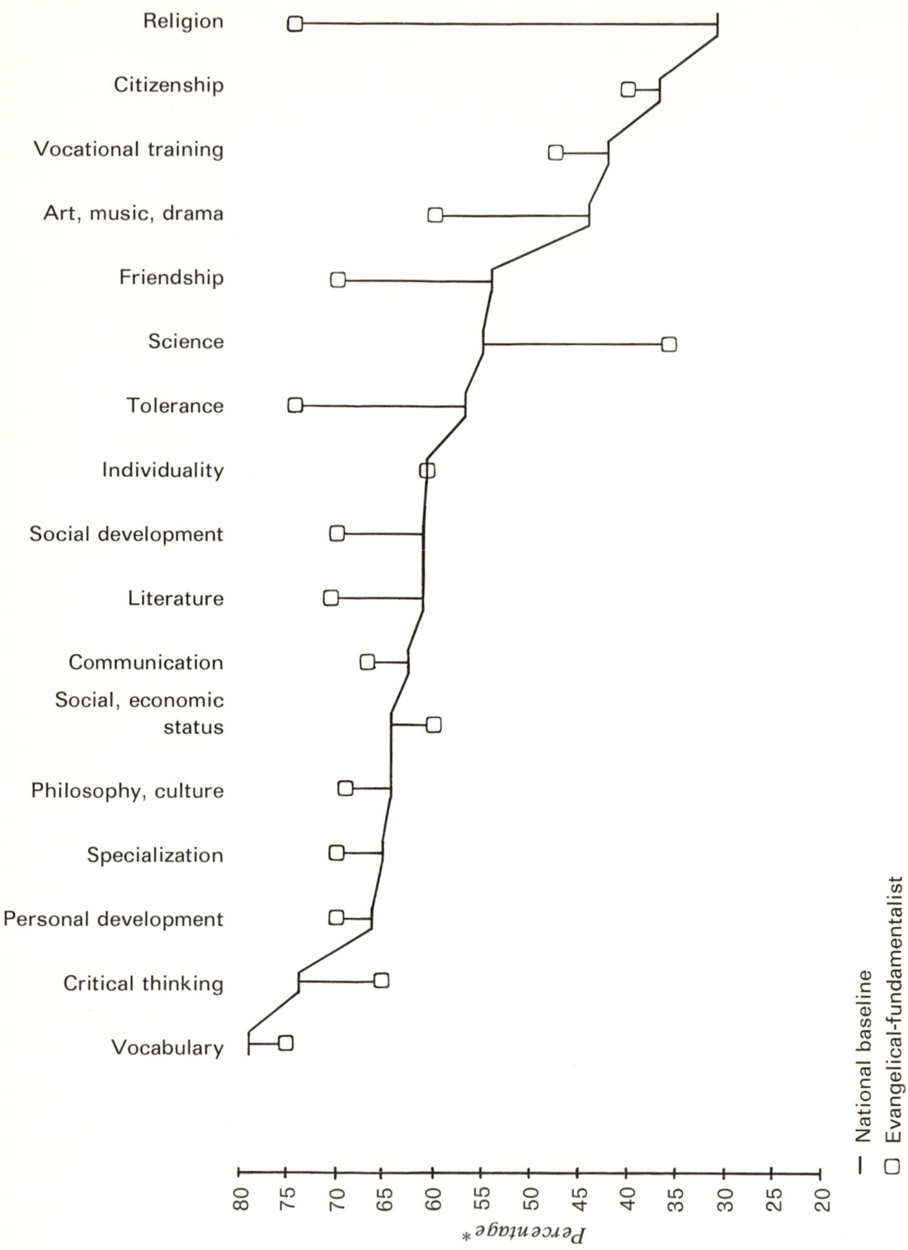

FIGURE 14 *Educational benefits: national baseline versus evangelical-fundamentalist; self-estimates of progress by alumni*

| National baseline
☐ Evangelical-fundamentalist

* Percentage marking "very much" or "quite a bit" of progress or influence.

colleges and other kinds of colleges. What we do have are 19 liberal arts colleges, associated in varying degrees with Protestantism: these 19 are part of a larger group of 74 colleges and universities. A small but randomly selected number of graduates from each of these colleges have reported the extent to which they believe they benefited or were influenced in various ways by their undergraduate college experience. From their reports it is obvious that the college influences reported by the Protestant college alumni are different in several respects from those reported by the more heterogeneous group of alumni that we have used as our national baseline. These influences are noticeably greater than the average with respect to an appreciation of religion, aesthetic sensitivity, tolerance and understanding of others, broadened literary acquaintance, social development, an awareness of different philosophies and ways of life, an understanding and interest in the style and quality of civic and political life, an appreciation of individuality and independence, and the development of lasting friendships and loyalties. The college influences are noticeably less than average with respect to vocational training and to an understanding of science and technology. Many of these influences may also be associated with a liberal education emphasis, or with liberal arts colleges as compared with universities, or with small colleges in small towns compared with urban multiversities. If so, then Protestant colleges share in these associations. Protestant college alumni attribute the same degree of influence as do alumni of other colleges to college experience related to the acquisition of facts, specialization, critical thinking, effective speech and writing, personal development, and improved social and economic status.

Not only are there Protestant college influences that differ from national average influences, there are also differences among the three sets of Protestant colleges. The dominant trend line runs from highest influence in Protestant-independent colleges, to lesser influence in mainline denominational colleges, and to least influence in evangelical-fundamentalist colleges on the following topics: critical thinking, awareness of different philosophies and ways of life, appreciation of individuality and independence, and understanding science and technology. Precisely the opposite trend line, with the evangelical and fundamentalist colleges having the greatest influence, occurs with respect to: appreciation of religion, vocational training, specialization, tolerance, and friendship. On all the other kinds of influence there are only small differences among the three groups of college alumni reports.

There is some similarity between these reported benefits and the previously reported characteristics of Protestant college environments. Environments described as friendly and supportive are surely compatible with influences in the direction of social development, tolerance, and friendships. So also the characteristics of propriety appear to be compatible with an appreciation of religion. The fact that critical thinking, an understanding of science, appreciation of different ways of life, and independence of thought and action are benefits more commonly cited by alumni of Protestant-independent colleges is consistent with their generally higher scores on awareness and scholarship. The fact that vocational training and specialization benefits are more commonly cited by alumni of evangelical-fundamentalist colleges is compatible with their generally higher scores on the practicality scale of CUES.

INVOLVEMENT IN CURRENT AFFAIRS

College graduates are contributors to and consumers of the culture in which they live. What they contribute and what they choose to consume are reflections of their interests and values. Our alumni survey questionnaire included a set of inventories of activity and interest in various aspects of contemporary affairs. Each inventory is a short test that provides a reliable score or index of involvement. The 11 inventories in the questionnaire relate to the following topics: community affairs, national and state politics, intercultural affairs, international affairs, art, literature, drama, music, education, religion, and science. The activities in each scale include some that are commonplace and easy to do and others that require more time and effort and a greater degree of personal or public commitment. The respondent is asked to check each activity he engaged in *during the past year.* The complete scales are reproduced in Appendix B.

In comparing Protestant college alumni with other college alumni we have arbitrarily established for each set of activities a national baseline that reflects more than a minimum level of involvement. Since the number of activities differs from one scale to the next, and since activities in the different scales are not equally easy or hard to do, we cannot conclude, from the number of activities checked, that people are more interested in music than in art, or in local community affairs than in international affairs. But we can clearly show the extent to which Protestant college graduates are more active, or less active, than the typical graduate from the 74 colleges and universities included in our national study.

In Figure 15 the horizontal line is the national baseline. It is labeled zero. The bars representing the three groups of Protestant colleges extend above or below this zero line. For example, on the community-affairs scale the Protestant-independent college alumni and the alumni of mainline denominational colleges are 5 percentage points above the zero line. The definition of "zero" for each topic is shown at the bottom of the chart. For community affairs it is defined as the percentage of the nationwide alumni group that checked 8 or more of the 12 activities in that scale, namely 44 percent. So, the first two Protestant groups are 5 percentage points higher (specifically $44 + 5 = 49$ percent checking 8 or more of the 12 activities) whereas the alumni from evangelical-fundamentalist colleges were 9 points lower (specifically $44 - 9 = 35$ percent checking 8 or more of the 12 activities).

The most common activities in each checklist are briefly noted in the next paragraphs to give more explicit meaning to the various scores.

With respect to community affairs (Com) nearly everyone talks about local problems, reads about local events in the paper, gives money to local charity, and votes in the local elections. Most alumni also belong to some community organization and contribute time or money to some civic projects.

In national and state politics (Pol) nearly everyone talks about politics, listens to speeches and discussions on TV, reads about political events in the papers, and votes in national and state elections.

Talking with friends about people and cultural events in other countries is the only common activity among those listed under intercultural (Icu).

With respect to international matters (Ina) nearly everyone reads newspapers and magazine articles about international relations and talks about foreign policy with friends and neighbors.

Talking about art (Art) and visiting a gallery or museum were the commonest activities related to art interests, but even these were checked by fewer than 60 percent of the graduates.

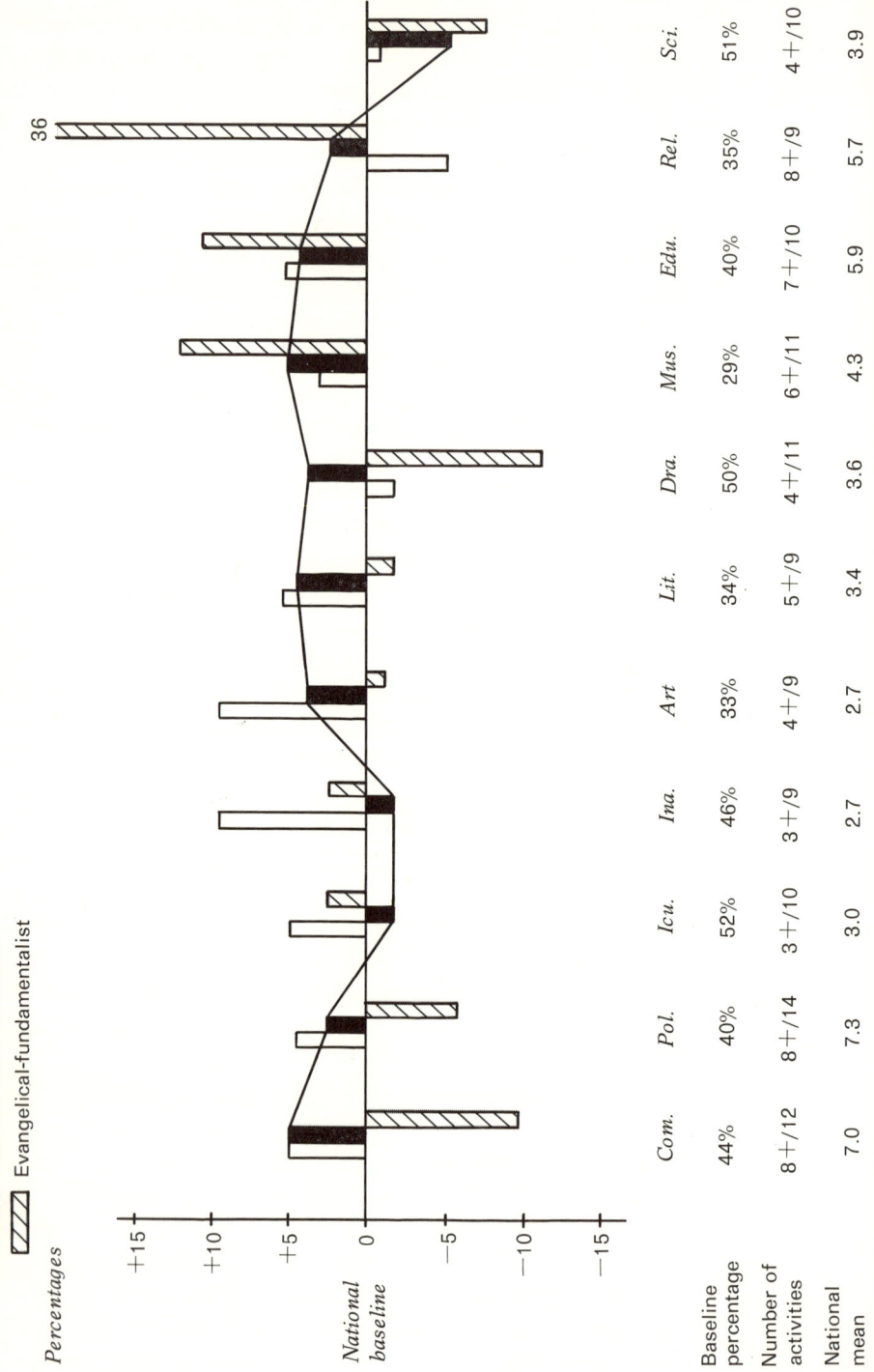

FIGURE 15 *Activities and interests: relative involvement of different groups of alumni*

In the checklist related to literature (Lit) the most common activities were buying books, talking about books, and reading book reviews and contemporary novels.

The most frequently checked items in the drama (Dra) category were watching TV dramas and talking about movies, plays, and TV dramas. A substantial majority also read theater and movie reviews and attended one or more plays.

Listening to the radio, buying phonograph records, and talking about music (Mus) were activities checked by a substantial majority of alumni. Reading music reviews and listening to serious music by contemporary composers were cited by close to a majority.

In relation to education (Edu) nearly everyone reported that he had talked about the schools, talked with a teacher or other official, visited a local school, read about education in the newspapers, and voted (or would vote) in favor of a bond issue or proposition to get more money for the schools.

Nearly all college graduates (more than three-fourths) reported that they went to church, belonged to a church, contributed a regular sum of money to a church, and read articles about church and religious activities (Rel).

Finally, in relation to science (Sci) more than three-fourths talk about it, read about new developments in research, and watch TV programs about science.

Alumni of the mainline denominational colleges appear to be quite similar to college graduates in general. In Figure 15 the solid bars with the connecting line between them are never more than 6 percentage points away from the baseline. With two exceptions this general similarity to the national baseline is also true of the alumni from the three Protestant-independent colleges. They do, however, get to 9 percentage points above the average in activities related to art and to international affairs.

As we have seen in other comparisons, it is again the evangelical-fundamentalist colleges that produce the most distinctive pattern. Their alumni are 36 points higher than the national baseline on the religious activity scale, with 71 percent of them engaging in eight or in all nine of the religious activities, as opposed to 35 percent of the national group and to 30 percent of alumni of the Protestant-independent colleges. The high involvement of evangelical-fundamentalist college graduates in activities related to education and to music may reflect the fact than many of them are teachers, preachers, or members of the church choir. Their lower than average amount of activity related to drama reflects the fact that they are less apt to go to movies or to see plays. No plausible explanation comes to mind to account for the lower level of activity in community affairs.

ATTITUDES ABOUT SOCIAL ISSUES

What do college graduates, and Protestant college graduates in particular, think about the society in which they are active participants? What do they think about the desirability of certain directions of social change and about some of the key issues that face the nation?

In a section of the questionnaire labeled "The Changing Society," we included a number of statements purporting to describe changes or trends that may or may not be occurring in the United States. We asked the alumni to indicate whether they thought the change or trend described by the statement was actually occurring. Then, for some of the statements, we also asked them to indicate whether the change described would be desirable or undesirable, if it in fact occurred or was in the process of occurring. The first response provides a measure of knowledge or awareness about the society (or at least an indicator of what people believe is happening in it). The second response is a measure of values, indicating whether the alumni are favorably or unfavorably disposed toward certain directions of change.

In presenting these statements of trends we have arbitrarily grouped them in certain ways and have noted the percentage of all alumni included in the national baseline that responded "generally true" to each of the statements. There were so few and such small differences between these national baseline percentages and the percentages obtained from the groups of Protestant colleges that we have not included the latter percentages.

The first five statements are about personal and social values—participation, self-expression, relating to others, individual achievement, and leisure time.

A new style of politics, involving broader and more active participation at all levels, is emerging. (Generally true, 69 percent)

More people are coming to realize and accept the value of self-expression—for example, through the arts. (Generally true, 64 percent)

As our society develops, the capacity for interdependence (relating with others) may be valued more highly than the capacity for independence and self-reliance. (Generally true, 70 percent)

Less importance is being attached to the value of individual success and achievement than has been traditional in our society. (Generally true, 45 percent)

Except for scientists, professionals, and executives, the number of leisure hours (among waking hours) is becoming greater than the number of working hours for the bulk of the employed population. (Generally true, 76 percent)

The next set of statements is about government and business, with the presumed direction of change being toward greater collaboration and less competition—between governmental units, between businesses, and between government and business.

There is an increasing movement toward inter-city government embracing both urban and suburban areas, and adjacent cities. (Generally true, 68 percent)

Some business and industrial organizations are moving away from competitive relations toward more collaborative relations. (Generally true, 55 percent)

There is an emerging trend for major industries to regard their resources as belonging not just to them but to all of society. (Generally true, 36 percent)

There is a growing trend to coordinate major public and private services—for example in housing, transportation, etc. (Generally true, 75 percent)

Within the market sector of the economy, the activities of the larger enterprises are becoming increasingly international in scope. (Generally true, 90 percent)

Increasingly, government is controlling the markets for the most advanced industries. (Generally true, 62 percent)

The final two items deal with separate issues, although the item about scientists and government could fit in with the others that describe governmental and business relationships. The item about segregated neighborhoods could be regarded as another reflection of personal and social values described in the first set of items.

Scientists and professionals are having an increasingly important influence on economic and governmental policies. (Generally true, 84 percent)

There is a tendency for large neighborhoods to become more exclusive in the kinds of people who live in them—white middle-class suburbs as well as parts of the "inner city." (Generally true, 53 percent)

All the statements about social trends are regarded as generally true by at least some social analysts. All but two of these statements are regarded as generally true by a majority of college alumni. Almost a majority (45 percent) think that less importance is being attached to the value of individual success and achievement; and about a third (36 percent) think that there is an emerging trend in which major industries regard their resources as belonging to all of society.

Table 4 reports the attitudes of college graduates toward these trends. College graduates clearly approve of greater participation in politics and of self-expression through the arts. They clearly do not think that it would be desirable to have more leisure time,

TABLE 4 Attitudes of alumni toward the changing society

		Percentage of alumni indicating that the change would be desirable		
			Protestant Colleges	
Direction of Change	National baseline	Independent	Mainline	Evangelical
More participation in politics	83	86	84	79
More value of self-expression	76	80	77	76
More value for interdependence	36	31	39	45
Less value on individual achievement	17	22	19	19
More leisure hours	47	52	48	34
More intercity government	61	65	63	55
Less competition, more collaboration in business	30	32	34	30
Resources belong to everyone, not just to the owners	66	69	64	67
Coordination of public and private services	70	75	69	69
Business more international in scope	67	77	66	56
More government control of markets	13	15	12	11
More influence for scientists and professionals	68	68	67	62
More segregated neighborhoods*	60*	68*	60*	64*

*Percentages for this item indicate a belief that the trend is, or would be, *undesirable.*

to value interdependence more than self-reliance, or to attach less importance to the value of individual success. The graduates of the evangelical-fundamentalist colleges are more likely than others to value the capacity for interdependence. They are also much less likely than others to think that greater leisure is desirable. The Devil finds work for idle hands, perhaps.

With respect to government and business, the attitudes of college graduates seem to be generally pro-business and pro-competition. If it is true that some businesses and industrial organizations are moving toward more collaborative relations, then most of these college graduates think that is undesirable. And if government is controlling the markets for the most advanced industries, that too is surely undesirable. On the other hand, coordination of major public and private services is desirable, and so is a trend toward larger governmental jurisdictions to coordinate cities and suburbs. Graduates of the evangelical-fundamentalist colleges are a bit more inclined than others to feel that bigness may be badness—55 percent think intercity government is desirable, compared with 65 percent among the graduates of Protestant-independent colleges; and 56 percent think the increasing international scope of business is desirable, compared with 77 percent of the graduates of Protestant-independent colleges.

Compared with other groups, a somewhat smaller percentage of graduates from the evangelical-fundamentalist colleges think that an increasing influence on governmental and economic policies by scientists and professionals is desirable.

Further insight regarding attitudes toward these postulated social trends may be gained by examining the graduates' viewpoints on certain current social problems and policies (Table 5).

The first four statements tap viewpoints about the government and national security. In general, the higher the percentages responding in the indicated direction, the stronger the support there is for world government, mutual trust, and interdependence. The lower the percentages, the more support there is for the virtue of self-sufficiency, independence, and peace through the imposition of superior power. It is clear that alumni of evangelical-fundamentalist colleges are more prone toward the latter set of views. *My God, right or wrong,* seems to go with *my country, right or wrong.*

With respect to the four viewpoints about women, again it is obvious that graduates of evangelical-fundamentalist colleges

TABLE 5 *Alumni viewpoints about social problems and policies*

	Percentage of alumni responding as indicated			
	National baseline	*Protestant Colleges*		
Viewpoints		*Independent*	*Mainline*	*Evangelical*
Government planning should be strictly limited, for it almost inevitably results in the loss of essential liberty and freedom. (Disagree)	45	47	47	38
We are not likely to have lasting peace unless the United States and its allies are stronger than all the other countries. (Disagree)	42	52	48	47
The United Nations should have the right to make decisions that would bind members to a course of action. (Agree)	62	67	67	54
The United States has enough natural resources and scientific know-how to be economically self-sufficient. (Disagree)	63	63	65	57
More women should be involved in policy formation both in business and in government. (Agree)	54	61	52	46
Professional women should have the same benefits and opportunities as their male colleagues. (Agree)	90	90	90	85
Being a housewife provides many opportunities to apply broad and creative interests. (Disagree)	22	25	20	15
Family patterns and attitudes should allow, and often encourage, married women to follow their own interests, even if they have young children. (Agree)	69	76	72	59
If Negroes live poorly, it is in great part the fault of discrimination and neglect from whites. (Agree)	50	61	52	48

Viewpoints	Percentage of alumni responding as indicated			
	National baseline	Protestant Colleges		
		Independent	Mainline	Evangelical
Anyone, no matter what his color, who is willing to work hard, can get ahead in life. (Disagree)	33	43	35	38
More money and effort should be spent on education, welfare, and self-help programs for the culturally disadvantaged. (Agree)	66	67	68	69
Issues such as law and order, civil rights, and public demonstrations are complex and need careful evaluation and judgment of individual cases. (Agree)	84	84	83	85
People who advocate unpopular or extreme ideas should be allowed to speak on college campuses if the students want to hear them. (Agree)	58	72	61	42
Literature should not question the basic moral concepts of society. (Disagree)	81	88	83	71

are the least likely supporters of women's liberation, feeling rather that woman's place is in the home. It is not that they are really antifeminist, it is just that they are more so than alumni of other groups of colleges.

Civil rights, freedom of advocacy, and social criticism are the topics of the remaining items. Graduates of the three Protestant-independent colleges are most willing to accept blame for discrimination against blacks, and are most likely to believe that not even hard work can overcome the handicaps of prejudice and that free speech and basic social criticism should not be interfered with. In contrast, graduates of evangelical-fundamentalist colleges are least willing to accept the charge of white racism and are least willing to condone free expression if it advocates unpopular or extreme ideas or if it is critical of basic moral concepts.

The differences reported in Table 5 are shown graphically in Figure 16. For example, on 10 of the 13 viewpoints the re-

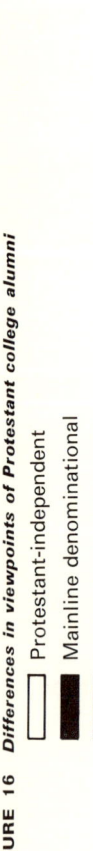

FIGURE 16 *Differences in viewpoints of Protestant college alumni*

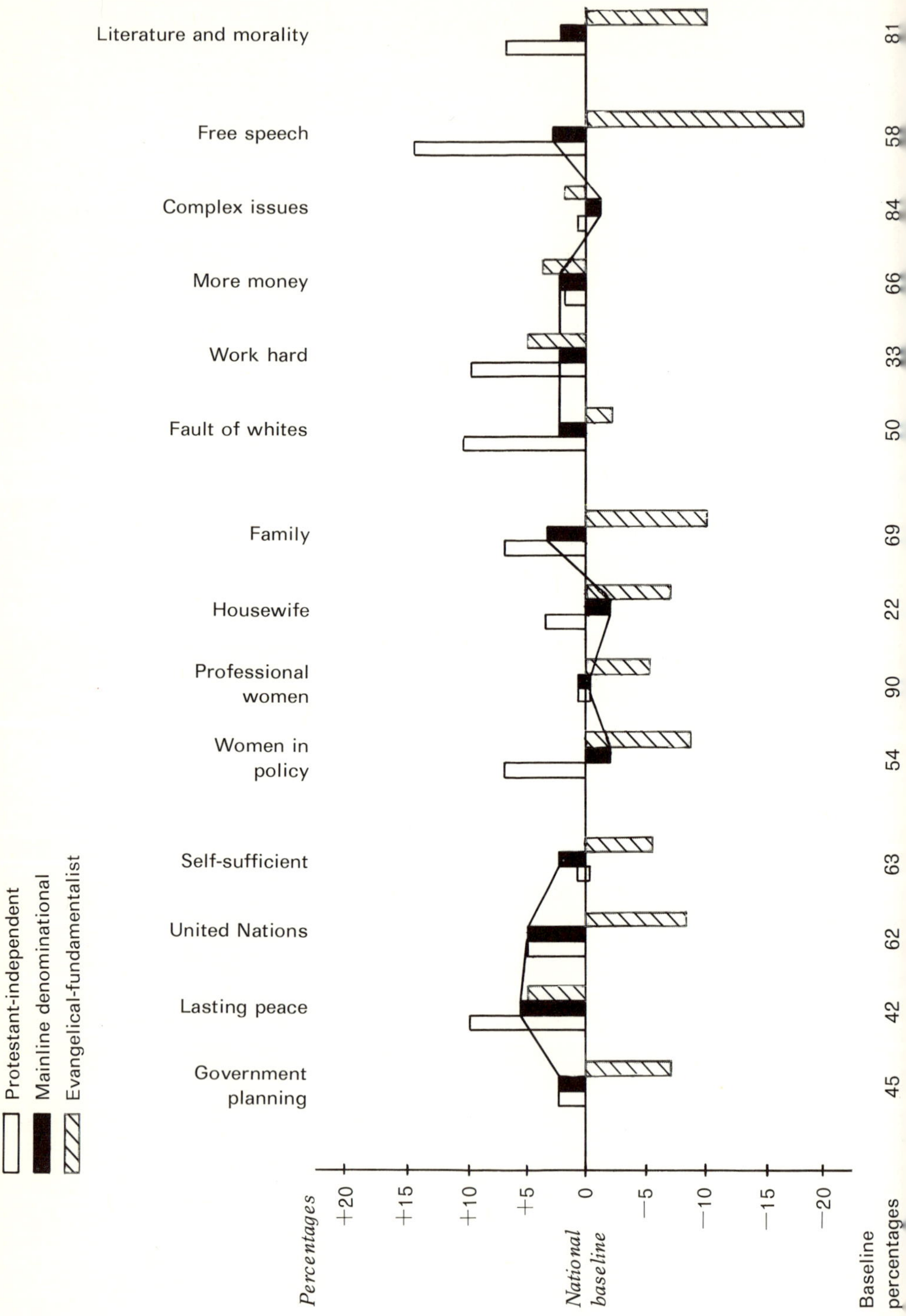

sponses of evangelical-fundamentalist college alumni are below the line for the national average. The differences are most extreme on the two issues regarding freedom of expression, the ones portrayed at the right-hand side of the graph. On the other hand, the responses of alumni from Protestant-independent colleges are above the national average on 10 of the 13 issues. Graduates of mainline denominational schools are close to the national average on all issues, although slightly above rather than below on 10 of the 13 topics.

PERSONAL TRAITS AND STATUS

In many respects the 1950 graduates of the 19 Protestant-related colleges are no different, on the average, from the total group of graduates from the 74 colleges and universities. Today, they typically live in small towns or cities of under 500,000; a majority describe themselves as Republican; about 30 percent of the men classify their occupations as managerial or executive. One thinks of students who go to private colleges as being a rather small minority; but in 1950 this was not true. At mid-century there were as many students in private institutions as in public ones; and among the private institutions a majority had some religious connection. It is not surprising, then, that the Protestant college graduates we have studied, and particularly those from colleges affiliated with the mainline denominations, are rather typical of graduates in general. In fact, the percentages reported for our sample of mainline college graduates were within 5 percentage points of, or closer to, the corresponding percentages for the total sample on 7 of the 17 educational benefits items, 9 of the 11 activity scales, all 13 of the attitudes toward social trends, and 13 of the 14 viewpoints on social problems and policies.

In Figure 17 we have summarized the attitudes and viewpoints about the changing society and various social problems and policies by combining the results into scores. We have also added to the chart some information about personal traits, status, and attitudes toward college.

The personal traits of autonomy and complexity are self-descriptions. Autonomy is defined as a general independence of traditional authority. The definition is inferred from self-descriptions of being adaptable and permissive, for example, rather than dutiful and conventional. It is also inferred from not liking such characteristics as "unquestioning obedience," or "the tried and the true." Complexity is defined as a tolerance for ambiguous

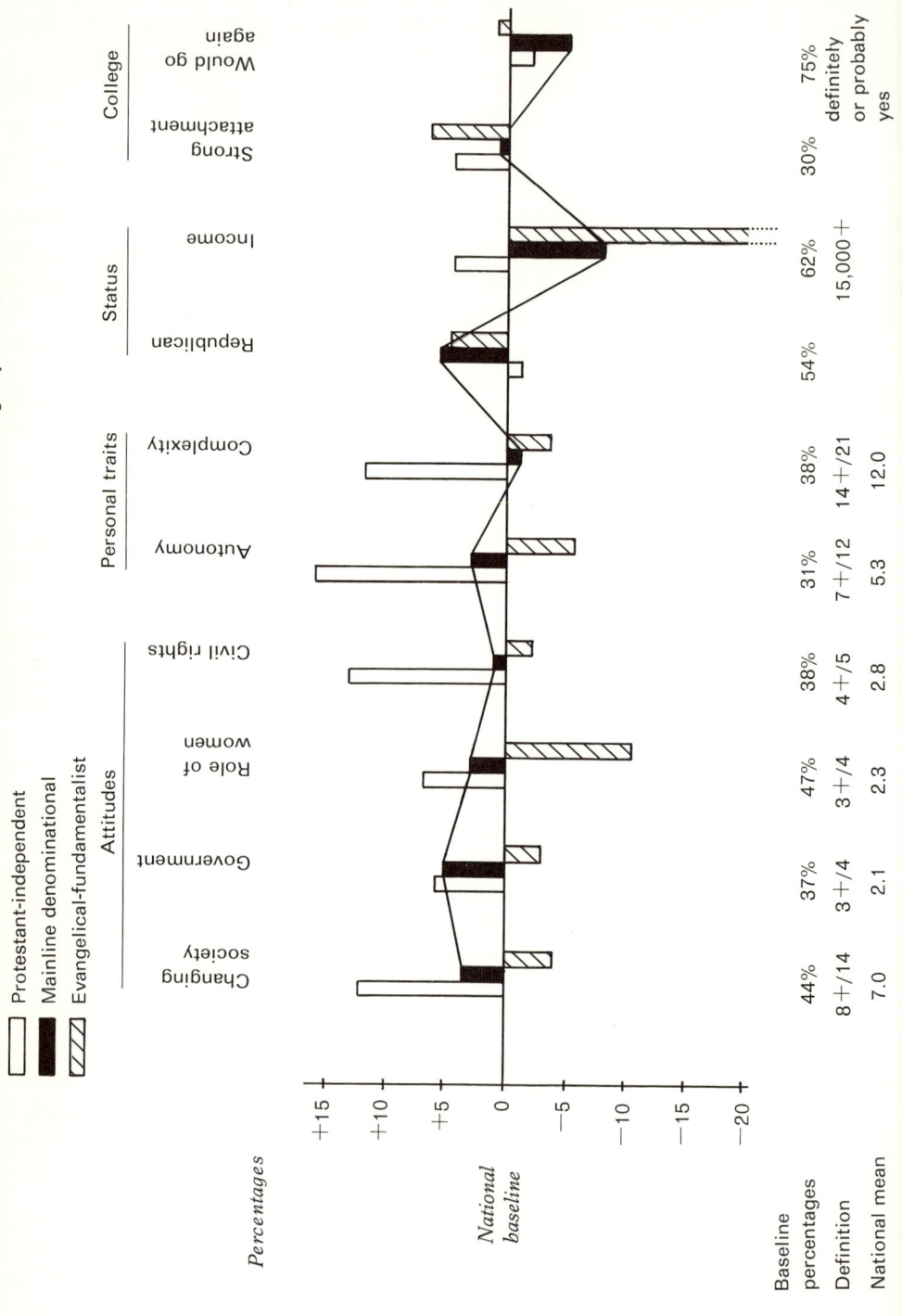

FIGURE 17 Attitudes, traits, status, and attachment to college: relative characteristics of different groups of alumni

situations and an enjoyment of dealing with complex and novel ideas. That is, one would describe himself as individualistic, open-minded, introspective, and experimental rather than as practical, predictable, and well-organized; and he would like original work, novel experiences, and dealing with new or strange ideas rather than predictable outcomes, a set schedule of activities, or straightforward reasoning. The questionnaire included 12 items presumably related to the trait of autonomy and 21 items related to the trait of complexity. These items are not a standardized or validated personality measure, although they are intended to be similar to such measures. We are not concerned with character sketches or personality descriptions as such; we are interested only in whether our various groups of alumni differ from one another in the ways they describe themselves. The answer is that they do. Thirty-one percent of the national group checked seven or more of the items presumably indicative of autonomy; forty-four percent of the alumni from the three Protestant-independent colleges checked seven or more of the items; thirty-four percent of the alumni of mainline Protestant colleges and twenty-five percent from the evangelical-fundamentalist colleges checked seven or more of these items. A similar pattern of differences, although not as great, is shown with respect to the presumed measure of complexity.

The next two items on the chart (Figure 17) show that a somewhat higher percentage of the mainline and evangelical college graduates, 60 percent and 59 percent respectively, identify themselves as Republican, compared with the national baseline of 54 percent, and the Protestant-independent college alumni report of 53 percent. As for economic status, defined as total family income, the baseline shows 62 percent reporting a figure of $15,000 or more (1969). In contrast, only 37 percent of evangelical-fundamentalist college alumni reported incomes higher than $15,000. This rather large difference reflects the fact that fewer alumni of these colleges enter managerial and executive occupations and proportionately greater numbers enter teaching and preaching.

As the alumni look back today on their experience at college, roughly a third (30 percent) say that they feel a strong attachment to the college (last two items of Figure 17). Graduates of the most religious colleges are more likely to feel a strong attachment, 37 percent, and so are graduates of the least religious colleges, 34 percent. We should add that 80 percent of all our college graduates say that their present feeling about their college is either "a strong attachment" or "pleasantly nostalgic"; and only 4 percent of our nationwide group said that their feelings were generally or thoroughly negative. When asked whether they would go to the same college if they could do it over again, three-fourths said definitely or probably yes. None of the three Protestant groups of alumni differed by more than 5 percentage points from this national figure. Nationwide, only 6 percent said "definitely no."

SOME PERSONAL EXPRESSIONS

Before we turn, in Chapter 5, to an examination of students currently in Protestant colleges, perhaps we should listen to the concerns, apprehensions, and hopes held by Protestant college alumni about higher education and youth today, and about the broader society.

On the last page of our questionnaire we invited the respondents to comment about themselves, their college, the society in general, or the questionnaire they had just answered. About a third responded to the invitation. From their responses we have selected for quotation some comments about higher education and about society in general. These were not the commonest comments. Most respondents said they enjoyed answering the questionnaire, found it a stimulation for self-appraisal, hoped that the results would be helpful and beneficial to higher education, and said that they would look forward to reading about the results. There were twice as many comments to that effect as there were on any other theme. The main secondary theme, however, was one of concern about today's youth; and it is on this theme that we have selected the following quotations.

The section of the questionnaire on the changing society was full of observations that pointed to one general direction—socialism.

The prevalent down-grading of ancient standards, and especially the espousing of relativism, is already having its natural result in the rising crime rate, student unrest, and general decline in morality.

A permissive culture rejecting moral absolutes and reasonable restrictions appears to have sown and reaped a generation of utterly confused people.

I see very little future for the colleges until someone sets the students straight and returns to the old-fashioned rule that professors should be obeyed. There is such a thing as too much tolerance and freedom.

I'd like to see more patriotism and loyalty to our country and our obligation and devotion to our God taught in schools generally.

Colleges must and should continue to be run, taught, and administered by the responsible adult individuals appointed by the lawful directive bodies. Disruptive and destructive militants should be held answerable for any and all breaches of the peace and breaking of the law.

The college has become too liberal for my thinking.

The strong attachment that I feel for my undergraduate institution is probably lessening as I observe changes in the character of the institution. This could affect my feelings relative to financial support in the future.

As a parent, one of the prime things I intend to look for in a college is one that will offer a full education without allowing violent and rebellious interruptions from a minority group.

I am unhappy about increasing role of federal government in our everyday lives; concerned about inflation, rising cost of living, and loss of buying power; concerned about destruction of national resources and increased detrimental effects of pollution of air and streams; proud of growth and expansion of schools and colleges (especially _____ College); appalled at lack of respect for law and order; disgusted with 90 percent of motion pictures shown in theaters and about 50 percent of television.

We need to help young people believe in something, if they can't they will fall for anything; and a belief in an absolute being who loves, forgives, and understands is a pretty good place to start.

Sometimes I think a large university might have provided me with better training in my field or helped me to find a different vocation which I might have liked as well as, or better than, teaching. However, recent contacts with individuals who had received only professional training and lacked any liberal arts courses have led me to wonder if the liberal arts background doesn't make one a more interesting, well-rounded and broad-minded person.

I do not think that I would have attended college had there not been a GI Bill of Rights. Conversely, I appreciated graduate school more than undergraduate for the major reason that *I* was paying for it.

I came from a very poor family. I attended college under the GI Bill of Rights without which I would never have been able to attend. I feel very strongly that everyone should have an opportunity to attend college. I have come into the world with nothing and will certainly take nothing with me when I leave, so if my children have been educated I will leave all I have to _____ College.

America, especially, needs some other value system for success besides money. Many of the most valuable pursuits, important work necessary to this society, do not pay nearly what they should; teachers, writers, researchers, ministers, and social scientists starve, while entertainers, stock brokers, diamond merchants, land salesmen, and money lenders grow rich.

Let us listen to the ideas and suggestions of the younger generation regarding their feelings and opinions toward their futures and help them *work* for and reach their goals.

I have a strong and growing investment in changing our educational institutions into more humanized places which are primarily concerned with the realization of human potential—not the development of components to fit the needs of our presently screwed-up priorities—industrially, politically, or socially.

Our American system has been unique in that the ordinary man can really improve his lot. For this society to survive, a sense of self-esteem and self-sufficiency must be felt by each American. These personal values must be related to a sense of world community also. But any schemes which depersonalize or demean the individual are undesirable.

I believe a greater effort should be made to bring the man in the street, particularly the one who has not attended college, into intimate contact with college people and activities. Not that he's excluded, but he thinks he is. The discipline of education thinking will help him see through some of his prejudices and superficial analyses of current issues. And on the other hand, such contact could help many college people understand the practical point of view of the family and job-oriented person, and to realize that he is not just a working machine that provides us with life's necessities, but a feeling, questioning, dissenting individual, too. In fact, they might even conclude that they need him more than he needs them.

I am pessimistic that any great changes can be made—our educational system is so firmly in the hands of those concerned with the economics (business) of education rather than what is needed by the students to live in today's society. No wonder the young people are dissatisfied. I am, too.

While the quality of the courses was important to me, even more significant was the total quality of life—as human beings dealt with one another.

Since many of these former students seem to think that today's students, with their rebellious and nonconformist attitudes and behavior, are a major social and educational problem, let us turn in the next chapter to an exploration of what today's students in Protestant colleges are really like.

5. The Students

In the spring or fall of 1969 a questionnaire identical in most respects to the one filled out by the alumni was given to upperclassmen at most of the colleges that had participated in the alumni survey, plus some added colleges (College Student Survey, 1969). Those who received the questionnaire in the spring were juniors; those who filled it out in the fall were then beginning their senior year. During the summer, or at the beginning of the fall term, most of these same colleges also administered a parallel questionnaire to incoming freshmen. The sample of students tested at each college was intended to be, and in most cases was, reasonably representative or random. Samples of 150 freshmen and 100 upperclassmen were requested from colleges with undergraduate enrollments of less than 5,000. The requested size of the sample was doubled for larger institutions. Returns were approximately 70 percent from the upperclassman samples and 80 percent from the freshman samples. The national baseline for the upperclassman survey includes approximately 7,300 students from 80 colleges and universities. Of the 74 colleges and universities composing the national baseline for the alumni survey, 67 also participated in the survey of upperclassmen and 59 in the survey of freshmen. In general, the types of colleges and universities added to the national baselines for upperclassmen and for freshmen were similar to ones that had been dropped.

Our focus in this chapter is on the upperclassmen — students who had been on the campus for three years at the time they responded to our questionnaire. All of them, with perhaps a few exceptions, would have graduated from college in June 1970. The Protestant-related colleges whose students we shall be describing are 16 of the same 19 whose alumni we described in the last chapter. The three colleges not included in our student analyses are Drew, Denison, and Westmont.

From the alumni survey we pointed out that 63 percent of the national baseline group identified themselves as Protestants; and that of the alumni from the 19 Protestant colleges we studied in detail, 82 percent said they were Protestant. In the next generation, roughly 20 years younger than the alumni, we find that 50 percent of the national upperclassman baseline identified themselves as Protestant; and that 62 percent of the students in the 16 Protestant colleges said they were Protestant. What primarily accounts for the difference is an increase in the percentage who say they have "no definite religious beliefs" or identify with "no formal religion." In any case, we begin this chapter by noting that Protestant colleges are not as Protestant as they used to be. In fact, among the three colleges we previously classified as "Protestant-independent" not even a majority of the students identify themselves as Protestant, the number saying "Protestant" (about a third) being equaled by the number saying "no definite beliefs" or "no formal religion." The justification for our continuing to classify the three colleges as "Protestant-independent" is the value of continuity and comparison with alumni, not in the continued validity of the label—although the label is still valid in the sense that among those who do state a religious identification by far the greatest proportion state "Protestant." Only in the evangelical-fundamentalist colleges do most students identify themselves as Protestant—practically 100 percent at Concordia and Goshen. The average for this set of four colleges is 85 percent, and it would be higher than 90 percent except that Pepperdine, which serves a rather varied clientele because of its location in an urban area and its openness to service in that area, had 64 percent of its upperclassmen stating "Protestant." Among the nine colleges we have classified as mainline denominational, a composite average of 61 percent of upperclassmen reported themselves as Protestant, the individual college percentage ranging from 52 to 81 percent.

PROGRESS TOWARD THE ATTAINMENT OF EDUCATIONAL BENEFITS

The content of the "Educational Benefits" part of the questionnaire for upperclassmen is identical to the alumni questionnaire, with only the following slight modification in the introduction: "In thinking over your experiences in college up to now, to what extent do you feel you have made progress or been benefited in each of the following respects?"

The answers are shown in Table 6. Since the statements are listed in rank order of "progress," one can readily see that the

TABLE 6 *Educational benefits: relative progress of different groups of upperclassmen*

	Percentage of upperclassmen indicating that they have made "very much" or "quite a bit" of progress			
	National baseline	Protestant Colleges		
Progress with respect to:		Independent	Mainline	Evangelical
Personal development	84	85	89	83
Tolerance	79	79	83	84
Individuality	76	80	81	74
Social development	75	79	78	73
Friendships	74	73	78	80
Critical thinking	71	73	71	65
Specialization	71	73	73	71
Vocabulary	69	68	68	63
Philosophy, cultures	69	84	75	71
Social, economic status	61	49	60	58
Literature	57	69	64	55
Art, music, drama	53	62	61	58
Communication	49	45	47	46
Science	43	37	37	32
Vocational training	40	17	32	55
Citizenship	36	38	37	29
Religion	35	32	36	70

first five all relate to human relations and interpersonal values, not to academic disciplines or methodologies. Moreover, the top five for the national baseline group are also the top five for each of the Protestant college groups—with the exception of one item for the Protestant-independent group. Comparing the responses to these five objectives or benefits with the corresponding ones from the alumni one sees that the percentages for the upperclassmen are from 12 to 22 points higher. Perhaps it is the immediacy of these human relations aspects of the college experience that accounts for the greater sense of benefit. On the other hand, it may be a reflection of the greater interest and value young people today place upon personal and social development—a genuine value difference between generations. Differences of 10 to 14 percentage points in the opposite direction occurred for three of the objectives—vocabulary, terminology, and facts in various fields of knowledge; understanding and appreciation of science and technology; and clear, correct, effective communication through writing and speaking. That students felt a lesser sense of progress toward these objectives may also reflect a generational difference—some disenchantment with science and technology, with the vocabulary of academic disciplines, and with linear modes of communication.

The extent to which students at Protestant colleges identify benefits in their college experience that differ from those claimed by students in general is shown in the next three charts. In Figure 18, comparing students at the three Protestant-independent colleges with the national baseline of upperclassmen at 81 colleges and universities, one finds that on only 5 of the 17 objectives is there any noticeable deviation. They report a much greater sense of progress toward the objectives of becoming aware of different philosophies and cultures, gaining a broadened literary acquaintance and appreciation, and gaining an appreciation of art, music, and drama. A much smaller percentage of students at the three colleges report progress toward the objectives related to vocational training and to improved social and economic status.

Even more striking is the extent to which students at the mainline denominational colleges are like students in general (Figure 19). On only 5 of the 17 objectives do their responses differ by more than 5 percentage points from the national baseline—and none of these is greater than 8 percentage points. To a somewhat greater extent than students in general, they express progress toward an awareness of different philosophies and cultures, a broadened literary acquaintance, and enjoyment of the arts; and to a somewhat lesser extent than students in general, they report progress toward the goal of vocational training and toward the goal of understanding science and technology.

Figure 20, which compares students at the four evangelical-fundamentalist colleges with the national baseline of upperclassmen, reveals differences of more than 5 percentage points on 7 of the 17 objectives. Clearly the greatest difference is with regard to the objectives of "appreciation of religion—moral and ethical standards," with 70 percent of the Protestant group reporting "very much" or "quite a bit" of progress in contrast to 35 percent for the baseline group. Substantially more of the Protestant group also report progress or benefit related to vocational training. The development of friendships and loyalties is also claimed by a somewhat higher percentage of students at the evangelical-fundamentalist colleges than by students in general. Four of the objectives or

The students 77

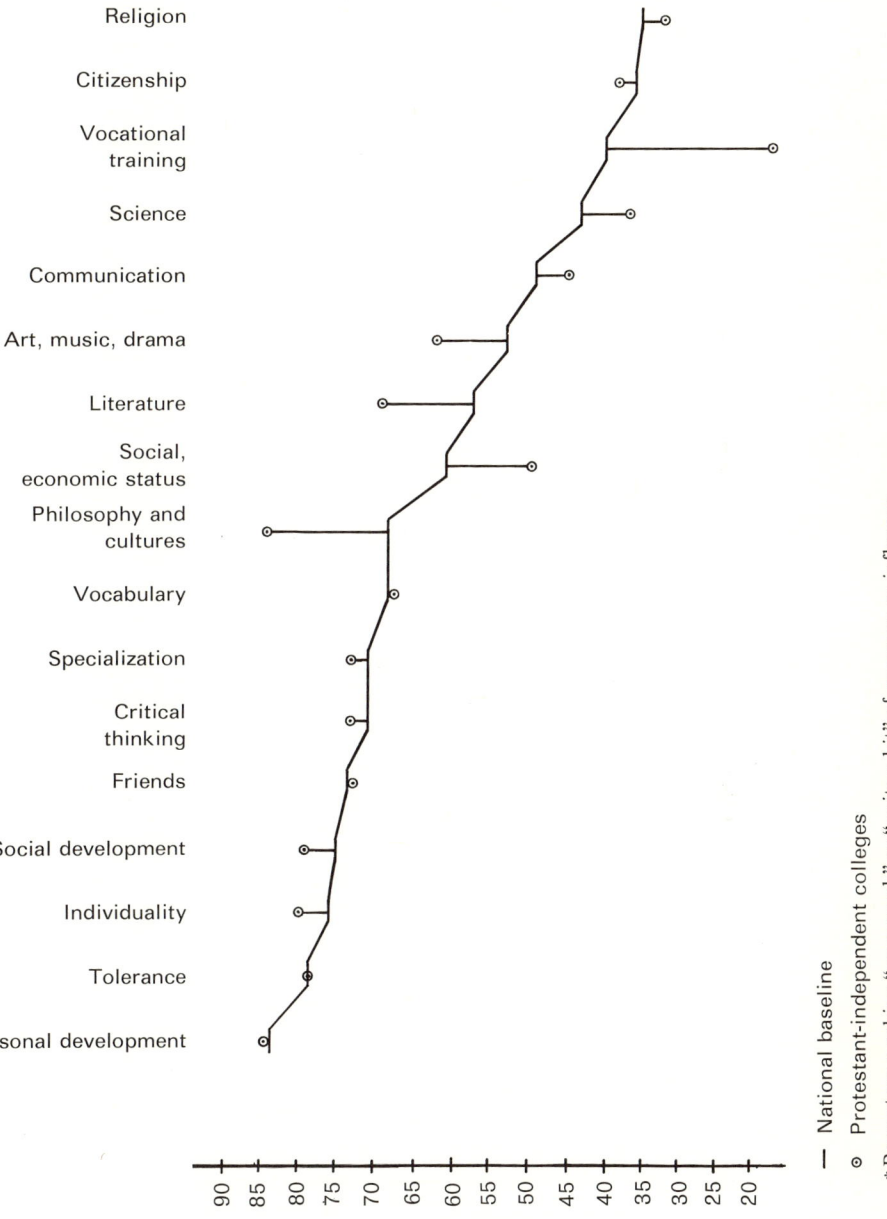

FIGURE 18 *Educational benefits: national baseline versus Protestant-independent colleges; self-estimates of progress by upperclassmen*

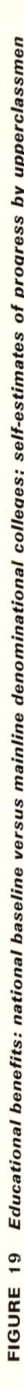

FIGURE 19 *Educational benefits: national baseline versus mainline denominational colleges; self-estimates of progress by upperclassmen*

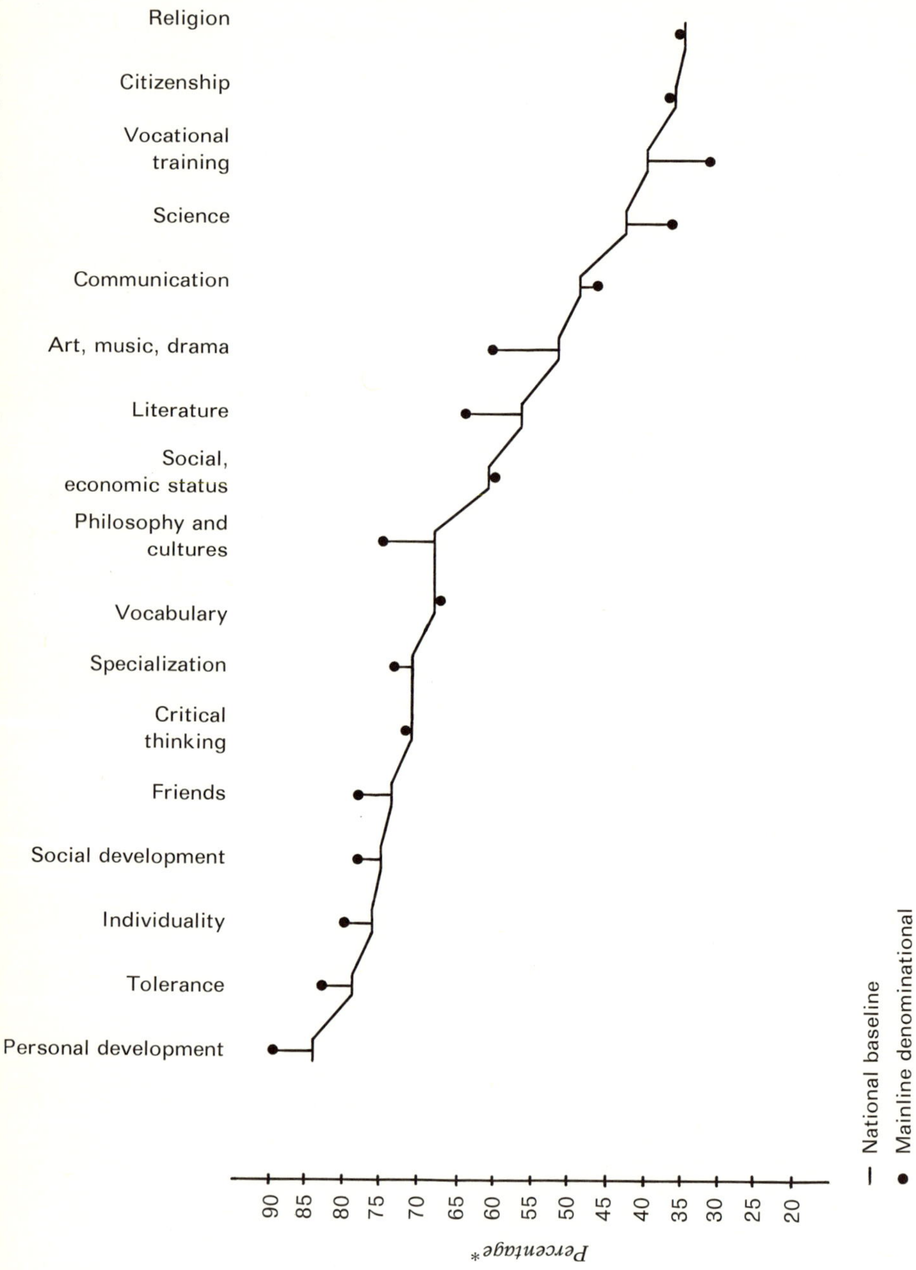

— National baseline
● Mainline denominational
*Percentage marking "very much" or "quite a bit" of progress or influence.

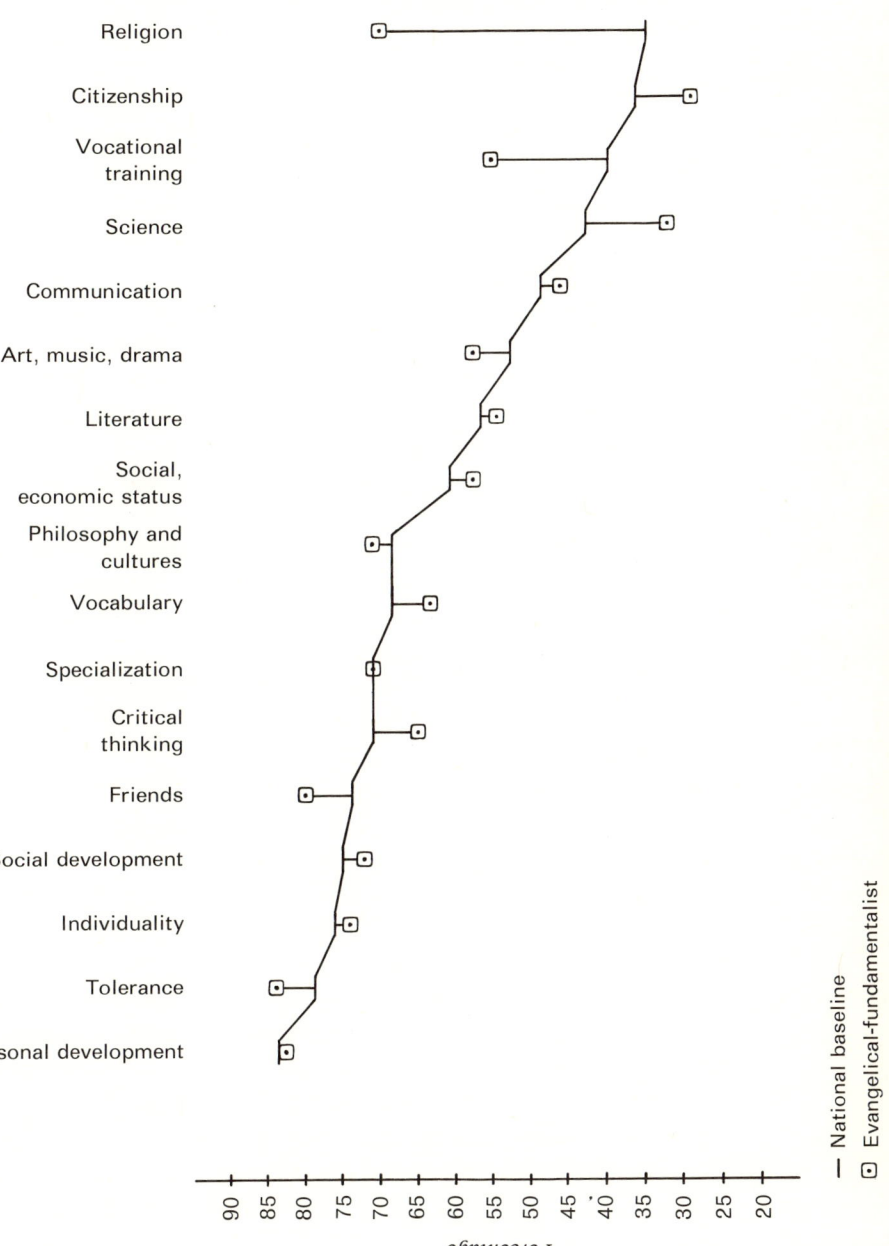

FIGURE 20 *Educational benefits: national baseline versus evangelical-fundamentalist colleges; self-estimates of progress by upperclassmen*

benefits show deviations in the opposite direction from the national baseline—with smaller percentages of students at the evangelical-fundamentalist schools reporting "very much" or "quite a bit" of progress toward the objectives related to critical thinking, vocabulary and facts, science, and citizenship.

The two main differences among the three groups of Protestant college students are, first, the much higher percentage of students from the evangelical-fundamentalist colleges stating benefits related to religion (which one would surely expect), and second, the higher percentage of evangelical-fundamentalist college students noting benefits related to specific vocational training (a result owing partly to the fact that Concordia is devoted to training teachers). Two other differences are in the opposite direction: Awareness of different philosophies and cultures, and a broadened literary acquaintance are cited by smaller proportions of students at evangelical colleges than at other Protestant colleges.

ACTIVITIES AND INTERESTS

The various activity scales that were a part of the alumni questionnaire were also used, with some modification, in the upperclassman questionnaire. The scale labeled "Education" was omitted; and in the scales related to community affairs and to politics, items about voting were omitted, as were other adult activities such as belonging to the PTA or holding a public office. All other scales were identical to the ones used with alumni.

It would be inappropriate to make direct comparisons between the upperclassmen and the alumni on some of the scales. The number of activities chosen as the dividing points for reporting the percentages at or above that level is not always the same, nor, in the case of the community and politics scales, is the number of items the same.

One can, however, look at relative deviations from the national baseline percentages (Figure 21). Again it is the mainline denominational group that is generally closest to the national baseline. The percentages reflecting their activity levels do not fall more than 1 to 3 points below the national levels on any topic; and they are more than 5 percentage points above the "average" on only three—intercultural affairs, art, and music. In contrast, both the Protestant-independent group and the evangelical-fundamentalist group are distinctly different from the average on a majority of the scales. The contrasting position of these two groups is sharpest on the scale of activities related to religion. In addition, the upperclassmen at the

FIGURE 21 ***Activities and interests: relative involvement of different types of upperclassmen***

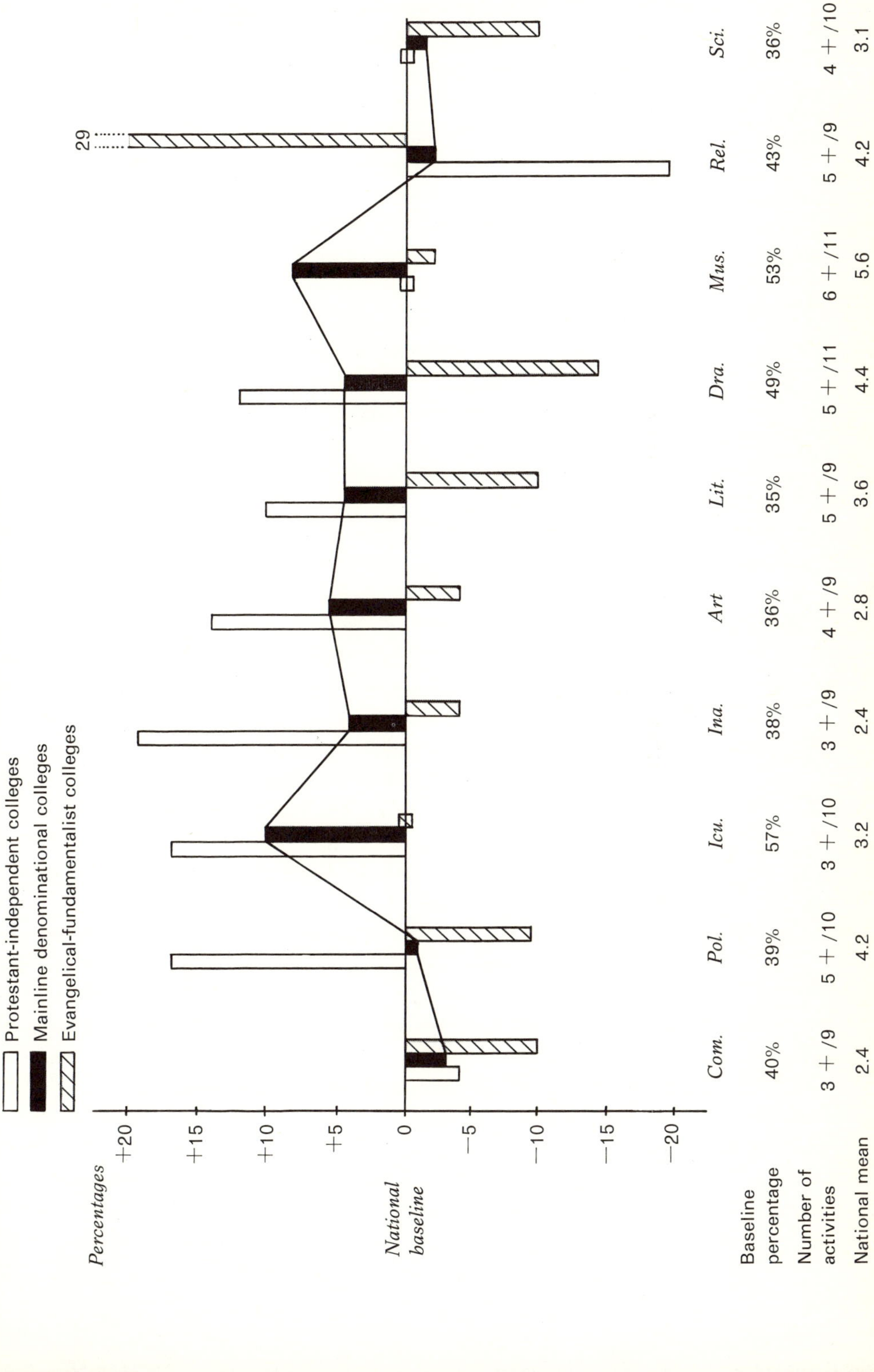
Protestant-independent colleges
Mainline denominational colleges
Evangelical-fundamentalist colleges
Percentages
+20
+15
+10
+5
0
−5
−10
−15
−20
National baseline
29
Com. *Pol.* *Icu.* *Ina.* *Art* *Lit.* *Dra.* *Mus.* *Rel.* *Sci.*
Baseline percentage 40% 39% 57% 38% 36% 35% 49% 53% 43% 36%
Number of activities 3 + /9 5 + /10 3 + /10 3 + /9 4 + /9 5 + /9 5 + /11 6 + /11 5 + /9 4 + /10
National mean 2.4 4.2 3.2 2.4 2.8 3.6 4.4 5.6 4.2 3.1

Protestant-independent schools have relatively more activities related to politics, intercultural affairs, international affairs, art, literature, and drama; and the upperclassmen at the evangelical-fundamentalist schools have relatively fewer activities related to community affairs, politics, literature, drama, and science.

Differences in the level of activity and interest among the three groups of upperclassmen are generally congruent with the differences among the alumni groups. The amount of deviation from the national baseline is typically greater in the student reports than in the alumni reports. As students, of course, they are reporting activities they have engaged in during the past year—and since nearly all the Protestant colleges we have studied are predominantly residential colleges, these activities would mainly be engaged in on the campus or in the college community.

ATTITUDES TOWARD SOCIAL CHANGE

The section of the questionnaire labeled "The Changing Society" was identical in both the alumni and the student surveys. Alumni responses are presented in Table 4. In comparing the responses of upperclassmen (Table 7) with those of alumni, we find what seems to us a rather remarkable similarity. Like the alumni, today's students strongly approve of social trends in the direction of more participation in politics, according greater value to self-expression through the arts, regarding resources as belonging to everyone rather than just to the owners, developing better coordination between major public and private services, and according increased influence to scientists and professionals. Like their elders, the students also disapprove of increasingly segregated neighborhoods, and of social trends that would minimize the virtues of individual achievement, lessen competition in business, or increase government control of markets.

Students in the evangelical-fundamentalist colleges, compared with other students, are most likely to disapprove of greater leisure time and most likely to approve of attributing greater value to the capacity for interdependence. They also have the lowest levels of approval for larger governmental units (intercity) and for more coordination between major public and private services. One does not get from these data any striking picture of a generation gap or any sharply unique set of views characteristic of students at the more evangelical-fundamentalist Protestant colleges.

When we look at viewpoints about more specific social problems rather than general social trends, we do find several clear differences between students and alumni. Table 8 reports student view-

TABLE 7 Attitudes of upperclassmen toward the changing society

	Percentage of upperclassmen indicating that the change would be desirable			
	National baseline	Protestant Colleges		
Direction of change:		Independent	Mainline	Evangelical
More participation in politics	80	85	80	74
More value of self-expression	82	83	80	84
More value for interdependence	40	40	44	56
Less value on individual achievement	26	33	24	28
More leisure hours	48	50	47	37
More intercity government	45	59	46	41
Less competition, more collaboration in business	31	36	30	36
Resources belong to every one, not just to the owners	64	69	62	63
Coordination of public and private services	70	77	73	62
Business more international in scope	57	48	59	58
More government control of markets	26	31	24	24
More influence for scientists and professionals	64	69	68	63
More segregated neighborhoods*	65*	79*	74*	69*

* Percentages for this item indicate belief that trend is, or would be, *undesirable*.

points on the same topics previously reported on for alumni in Table 5. There are five topics or issues about which young and old have noticeably different attitudes. Somewhat less than half (45 percent) of the alumni group disagreed with the proposition that "government planning should be strictly limited, for it almost inevitably results in the loss of essential liberty and freedom." Fifty-nine percent of the students disagreed with that proposition. Again, somewhat less than half of the alumni disagreed with the notion that lasting peace depends on the United States and its

TABLE 8 *Upperclassman viewpoints about social problems and policies*

	Percentage of upperclassmen responding as indicated			
	National baseline	*Protestant Colleges*		
Viewpoints		*Independent*	*Mainline*	*Evangelical*
Government planning should be strictly limited, for it almost inevitably results in the loss of essential liberty and freedom. (Disagree)	59	63	61	59
We are not likely to have lasting peace unless the United States and its allies are stronger than all the other countries. (Disagree)	64	81	72	69
The United Nations should have the right to make decisions that would bind members to a course of action. (Agree)	66	67	66	62
The United States has enough natural resources and scientific know-how to be economically self-sufficient. (Disagree)	59	58	64	54
More women should be involved in policy formation both in business and in government. (Agree)	52	52	48	51
Professional women should have the same benefits and opportunities as their male colleagues. (Agree)	88	88	86	86
Being a housewife provides many opportunities to apply broad and creative interests. (Disagree)	25	26	23	14
Family patterns and attitudes should allow, and often encourage, married women to follow their own interests, even if they have young children. (Agree)	65	67	68	57
If Negroes live poorly, it is in great part the fault of discrimination and neglect from whites. (Agree)	52	79	57	48

	Percentage of upperclassmen responding as indicated			
	National baseline	Protestant Colleges		
Viewpoints		Independent	Mainline	Evangelical
Anyone, no matter what his color, who is willing to work hard can get ahead in life. (Disagree)	46	72	56	49
More money and effort should be spent on education, welfare, and self-help programs for the culturally disadvantaged. (Agree)	76	89	80	81
Issues such as law and order, civil rights, and public demonstrations are complex and need careful evaluation and judgment of individual cases. (Agree)	89	94	89	87
People who advocate unpopular or extreme ideas should be allowed to speak on college campuses if the students want to hear them. (Agree)	86	94	92	76
Literature should not question the basic moral concepts of society. (Disagree)	88	98	93	84

allies being stronger than other countries; but two-thirds of the students (and even more of the Protestant college students) reject the concept of peace through superior force.

Nearly half the students, and more than half the Protestant college students, disagreed with the statement that "anyone, no matter what his color, who is willing to work hard can get ahead in life." A third of the alumni had disagreed with that statement. It appears that the younger generation is more skeptical about the validity of the Protestant work ethic—at least as it applies to minority groups. Also, three-fourths of the students (and even more of the Protestant students), compared with two-thirds of the alumni, think that "more money and effort should be spent on education, welfare, and self-help programs for the culturally disadvantaged."

The biggest difference between the viewpoints of students and adults is on the issue of free speech. Fifty-eight percent of the alumni

Education and evangelism 86

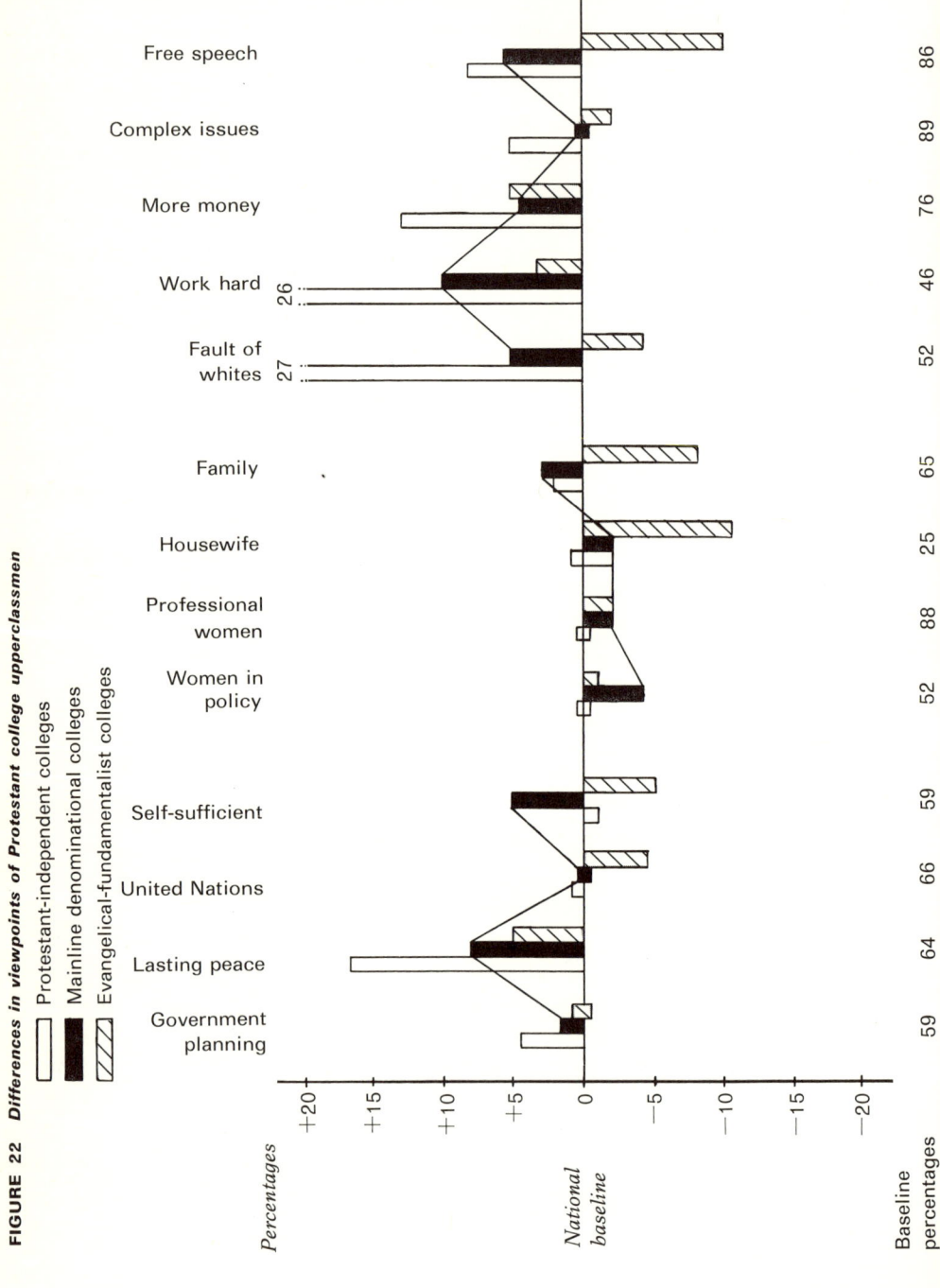

FIGURE 22 Differences in viewpoints of Protestant college upperclassmen

had agreed that "people who advocate unpopular or extreme ideas should be allowed to speak on college campuses if the students want to hear them." Eighty-six percent of the students expressed this attitude. Moreover, although not even a majority of alumni of evangelical-fundamentalist colleges had endorsed this free-speech statement, three-fourths of the students now at those colleges endorse it.

Differences in viewpoints among the Protestant college student groups are shown in Figure 22. The generally more "conservative" views of students at the evangelical-fundamentalist colleges are apparent. Their endorsement of two of the items related to the role of women is less than the national baseline group of students and so is their more limited endorsement for controversial campus speakers. The most deviant elements in the chart are the viewpoints of students at the Protestant-independent colleges. They overwhelmingly reject the concept of peace through strength; they are much more willing to blame whites for the poor status of Negroes; are much more skeptical of the notion that willingness and hard work can overcome the handicaps imposed by prejudice; are more willing to spend money to help the culturally disadvantaged; and are more receptive to free speech.

PERSONAL TRAITS AND STATUS

The various attitudes and viewpoints we have been discussing are summarized in Figure 23 as if they were a set of short tests, each yielding a score. The questionnaire contained 14 statements about the changing society that students were asked to mark either desirable or undesirable. The number of statements marked "desirable" is an indicator of the acceptability of changes that are presumed to be occurring. (The score is based on 14 items but we have considered only 13 of them in our text: the other item was regarded as occurring and as desirable by nearly everyone, 95 percent to 100 percent, so we do not discuss it. The item was "An increasing proportion of young people are graduating from high school and going to college.") The chart shows that 8 or more of these 14 trends were regarded as desirable by 47 percent of the upperclassmen in our survey; that more upperclassmen (9 percentage points more, or 56 percent) from the Protestant-independent colleges thought so; and that upperclassmen at the mainline denominational colleges and at the evangelical-fundamentalist colleges were about the same as the national baseline group. With respect to viewpoints about government, about the role of women, and about civil rights, the

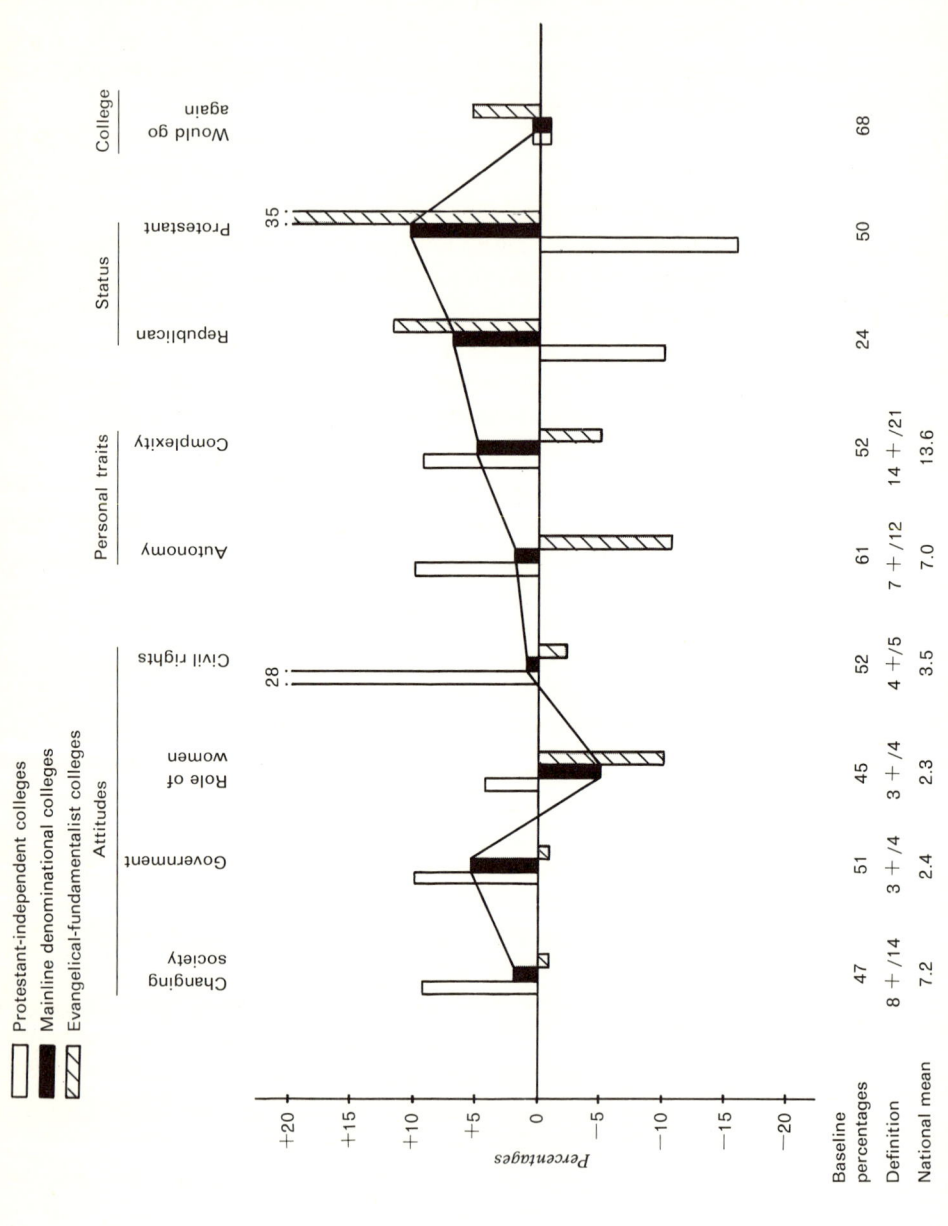

FIGURE 23 Attitudes, traits, status, and attachment to college: relative characteristics of different groups of upperclassmen

more "liberal" response from the upperclassmen at the Protestant-independent schools is clear, as is the more conservative response from evangelical-fundamentalist college upperclassmen regarding the role of women.

The two measures of personal traits also shown in Figure 23 are the same as those we described in the previous chapter. On both measures, autonomy and complexity, there is a substantial contrast between the students at the "modernist" colleges and the students at the "fundamentalist" colleges.

In political identification, greater proportions of students at the evangelical-fundamentalist colleges describe themselves as Republicans. The mainline group is also higher than the national average in this respect, whereas the Protestant-independent group contains fewer Republicans.

When asked "If you could start over again, would you go to the same college you are now attending," 68 percent of our national group of undergraduates said yes (either "yes, definitely" or "probably yes"). Protestant college upperclassmen feel the same way, with the exception that "yes" is a little more frequent among the evangelical-fundamentalist college students.

STUDENT PROFILES

We have taken some 54 measures of college students, most of which can be regarded as relevant to educational purposes and educated people. There were self-ratings of progress toward 17 objectives. There were measures of the level of activity and interest in 10 areas or aspects of society, each of which has some validity as an educational objective. There were 13 statements about potentially major social trends, with opportunity to judge their desirability. And there were 14 expressions of viewpoints about significant social issues and problems with which one could agree or disagree. As we have presented our survey results we have usually called attention to instances in which the groups of Protestant college students deviated by more than 5 percentage points from the national baseline. Overall, the results from the upperclassmen at the Protestant-independent colleges have deviated beyond this minimum level from the national baseline in 25 of the 54 measures, the mainline group in 11 of the 54, and the evangelical-fundamentalist group in 20 of the 54.

A profile of the ways in which students at the Protestant-independent colleges differ from students in general shows the following pattern. They express a greater sense of progress toward liberal arts and humanistic objectives—specifically philosophy, literature, and arts—and less progress toward the pragmatic objectives of vocational training and improved social and economic status. Their activities are more numerous in the fields of politics, international and intercultural affairs, art, literature, and drama; but the level of their religious activities is much lower. They are more accepting of social trends purported to encourage intercity government agencies and more coordination between major public and private services; but more skeptical about the desirability of business becoming more international in scope. They are more inclined to think that some reduction in the value placed on individual success and achievement would be desirable. To a greater than average degree they think it undesirable for neighborhoods to become more segregated. On the maintenance of peace in the world, they reject the notion that "we" have to be stronger than "the others." With respect to the status of blacks and other minorities in our society, their attitudes show a greater recognition that whites may be to blame for much of it, that not even hard work can always overcome the barriers imposed by prejudice, and that more money ought to be spent to help balance the scales. They are most insistent on their right to hear controversial speakers and on freedom from censorship in literature. In other personal characteristics they seem to possess a greater degree of autonomy and independence from traditional authority and to enjoy dealing with complexity, ambiguity, and novelty. And finally, compared with college students in general, fewer are Republican and fewer are Protestant.

The profile of students at the evangelical fundamentalist college is, in many respects, a contrasting one. They are less likely to express progress toward certain liberal arts and academic objectives —specifically critical thinking, vocabulary and facts, science and technology, and citizenship—and more likely to express greater progress toward the personal and practical goals of vocational training, friendship, and religion. Except for activities related to religion, which they engage in to a much greater extent than other students, their level of involvement in other areas is lower than average—specifically in community affairs, politics, literature, drama, and science. They are less accepting of social trends that purportedly would provide more leisure time, widen political participation, and bring about more coordination of public and private services; but they are more favorably inclined to recognize the importance of interdependence. With respect to various viewpoints, their attitudes toward women are more conservative or traditional, and their endorsement of the right to hear controversial speakers, although strong, is less strong than it is among students in general. On the measure of autonomy they are less autonomous and less independent of traditional authority than are students in general. And, finally, they are more solidly Republican and overwhelmingly Protestant.

Upperclassmen at the mainline denominational colleges differed in relatively few respects from upperclassmen in general. Rather than note these differences, we have elected to note the extent to which this "middle" group tends to be more like the Protestant-independent group or more like the evangelical-fundamentalist group.

In their progress toward various educational objectives, the mainline group is closer to the "independent" group on most of the liberal arts objectives—critical thinking, vocabulary, literature, arts, science, and citizenship. They are also closer to the independent group in the relatively low estimates of progress toward the objectives of vocational training and religion. Their answers are closer to those of the evangelical group with respect to the objectives of understanding philosophies and cultures, developing friendships, and improving their social and economic status.

The middle group is closer to the independent group in most of the activity measures—community affairs, intercultural affairs, literature, drama, music, religion, and science. They are closer to the evangelical group in activities related to art, politics, and international affairs.

In assessing the desirability of social trends, the middle group is closer to the independent group in welcoming broader political participation, more leisure time, and more coordination between public and private service; and in disapproving of segregated neighborhoods and in being more skeptical about the values of interdependence as opposed to self-reliance. Their views are closer to those of the evangelical group in valuing the importance of individual achievement and success, in the approval of more international scope for business, and in doubting the virtue of new levels of government to deal with intercity and city-suburban problems.

Their attitudes toward the role of women are closer to those of the independent group; and so are their attitudes regarding free speech and censorship. On world peace and civil rights, however, they are like the fundamentalist group. While they are skeptical of peace through strength, recognize the fault of whites for the poor status of minorities, feel that not even willing hard work can overcome the roadblocks to success imposed by prejudice, and that more money needs to be spent to help people who have been deprived—and while higher proportions of them hold these views than the proportion for students in general—their attitudes are not nearly as "liberal" as the attitudes of the Protestant-independent group.

With respect to the traits of autonomy and complexity, the middle group is closer to the independent group. With respect to the proportion of Republicans and of Protestants, the middle group is closer to the evangelical-fundamentalist group.

In adding up the box score to see on whose side the mainline denominational group most frequently falls, we count 24 measures putting them closer to the independent group and 13 measures putting them closer to the evangelical-fundamentalist group. There were 54 measures in all, but we did not count ones on which all the groups were within 5 percentage points either above or below the national baseline.

Given the data we have presented in this chapter, one would have to conclude that there is no "typical" Protestant college student. In an earlier chapter we saw that the environment of most Protestant colleges was rather similar to the environment of most liberal arts colleges, with the exception of the more strongly evangelical-fundamentalist college environments. Since an environment consists, among other things, of the people who live in it, one would expect distinctive environments and distinctive students to go together. And indeed there is a distinctiveness about students in the evangelical colleges that seems congruent with the distinctiveness of their college environment.

Except in the more evangelical colleges there has been a clear erosion of Protestant religious identification over the past three generations, as the following tabulation indicates.

Colleges	Percent saying they are Protestant			
	Parents of the alumni group	Alumni class of 1950	Parents of current students	Current upper-classmen
The Protestant-independent colleges	83	75	60	34
The mainline denominational colleges	84	78	79	61
The evangelical-fundamentalist colleges	94	93	88	85

The upperclassmen would be about 20 years old, their parents and the alumni of the class of 1950 would be 40 to 50 years old, and the parents of the alumni, if they were living, would be about 70 years old. We have, then, just about spanned the twentieth century up to this point. At the end of the next generation, by then approaching the twenty-first century, I suspect there will be little change in the evangelical-fundamentalist group. Eighty-five to ninety percent of their students and the parents of their students will be Protestants. What happens in the colleges affiliated with the mainline denominations is a more interesting and uncertain speculation. Will they be recognizable as Protestant colleges—either in the character of their student body or in the character of their environment?

6. *Impressions and Thoughts*

There is only so much one can learn by looking at an IBM card. Personal visits I made to 10 campuses during September 1970 have added to my appreciation, and perhaps to my understanding, of the topic of this book. My itinerary included Carleton, Macalester, Beloit, Albion, Goshen, Franklin, Denison, Wooster, Susquehanna, and Lycoming. The one school in this list that has not been mentioned in our earlier chapters is Carleton. Historically, Carleton has had some connection or cooperative relationship with the Congregational churches of Minnesota. In the Danforth report it is not listed as a church-sponsored college. Nonetheless, we have included it as a good example of what we have been calling Protestant-independent colleges. In writing to the presidents of the colleges, I described the purpose of my visit in rather general terms, indicating that I was not coming with a specific set of questions but rather with an open curiosity about the college (admissions, programs, finances, students, etc.), and to see and learn whatever they would like to show me or tell me about these or any other aspects of the campus, given the time restraints of a day's visit, which usually meant about five or six hours. Since my purpose now, in drawing upon the notes I made at the time of these visits, is not to characterize or judge these colleges or to describe my impressions of each of them, I have grouped my observations and comments under various topics.

IMPRESSIONS

Bricks and stones

At all the colleges I visited there were new buildings. Carleton had recently completed a fine arts building and was raising money for a new science building. Macalaster had a new science building, a new center for arts programs, and a new chapel. There was a large new chapel building at Goshen, also a large chapel at Susquehanna and one under construction at Wooster. Wooster also had a new student center, as did Franklin. Lycoming had a new academic center consisting of several interconnected buildings housing a variety of programs.

Most liberal arts colleges are made of red brick. How attractive that turns out to be depends partly on the setting, the shrubbery, the trees, and the ivy. Wooster is made of stone. In most cases the new buildings seem to be rather like the old, with some pleasant exceptions. The Wooster chapel, still under construction when I was there, impressed me as a splendid and dramatic building. The chapel at Macalaster is of wood and glass.

There is also a familiar feeling about most liberal arts campuses. Almost unerringly one can pick out the administration building and the chapel. And one senses at least part of the reason for the friendly atmosphere of the place, as so clearly emerged from student responses to the college environment scales: It really feels like a neighborhood, a place where one knows his neighbors, a place that can be comprehended. Whether the buildings seem rather spare and economical, as at Goshen, or more substantial and splendid, as at Wooster, they are generally well tended. I found it to be of some interest that fairly impressive chapel buildings were among the new additions at four of the campuses I visited.

Programs and special features

In some of my conversations I asked what it was about the college that seemed to attract students and whether there were any fairly recent changes in curriculum or other programs.

Many students come to Macalester, for example, because about 60 to 70 percent of them receive some kind of financial assistance. The school's nationwide program for recruiting National Merit Scholars has received annual contributions of about $1 million from DeWitt Wallace, who is the founder and publisher of *Reader's Digest,* and whose father, James Wallace, was a distinguished president of the college in its early days. One cannot, of course, successfully recruit lots of good students to an academically poor college. Considerable flexibility seems to exist in the Macalester program. The usual liberal arts distribution requirements have been drastically reduced: the student is required to take one course in science or mathematics, one course in social sciences, and two courses in humanities. Satisfactory-unsatisfactory grading exists wholly for the freshman year and partially in other years.

Each department has a student-faculty committee to advise the department on its instructional program and on the nature of the senior comprehensive examinations. There is an Inner College similar to experimental colleges on other campuses where student-initiated courses may be offered.

Beloit requires every student to have one semester off campus and most students opt for the overseas program. Macalester also gives students a chance to go abroad for a semester or on a summer work-study program. Goshen sends nearly all of its students to Carribbean and Central American countries for one semester.

An interesting innovation at Wooster is a freshman colloquium. All freshmen register for a course called Freshman Colloquium for the first quarter of the year. The colloquium is concerned with the critical discussion of ideas. Students are randomly distributed to sections, each of which is taught by a different faculty member, who is free to organize his group in any way he chooses. The faculty member serves as adviser to the approximately 15 freshmen in his section until each student identifies a major field and obtains an adviser in that field.

At Denison the general education program or distribution requirement seemed to be fairly traditional—adding up to some 36 units in science, social sciences, humanities, English, language, etc. However, there is also an experimental college that offers a variety of student-initiated nongraded courses. Some units of credit toward graduation can be taken in this college. Units of credit can also be gained by attending weekly convocation and chapel programs.

Susquehanna has an Environmental Studies Institute, apparently centering on a local watershed, more or less self-contained, where the students do a good bit of field work.

Black and white
"There just aren't any black people who live in Northfield, Minnesota." There are some black students at Carleton but it has been difficult to get black faculty members. There are about 40 to 50 black students at Albion, with another 20 or 25 expected in the freshman class—but no black faculty or staff members. They have had some and have tried to recruit others, but without much success. So they are working on a project for faculty exchanges with some Southern schools.

Macalester was the only school I visited that was located in a big city. It has an active recruiting program for black students and about 10 percent of the students, along with about 14 faculty members are black. Some people in the community feel that the college is going too far in trying to accommodate blacks and in becoming involved with social issues.

Wooster has new programs in urban studies, Afro-American studies, and Indian studies. It has about ninety black students, and also has four faculty members, one dean, and two administrative interns who are black. A new campus minister who recently came to the college from a ghetto area in Detroit was described to me as dynamic and liberal.

In a prior year Denison had a prolonged crisis with black students, which, I was told, rather severely polarized the campus. At one point the black students obtained from the admissions office the names of all black applicants and wrote to each of them advising them not to come to Denison and indicating that they themselves had no intention of returning the following year. Nearly all of them (about 40), however, did return and about 20 new students were successfully recruited. I do not know whether there have been further difficulties. I was told that the administration had appointed a new director of black studies who was previously a teacher in a Southern college, that his appointment was not favorably accepted by the black student organization, and that the new director had appointed an associate director without even consulting the black student organization. If these statements were correct, I would suppose that some difficulties would continue.

Student life
"There are really no rules about dormitory life on the campus. People do more or less what they want. However, because it is a relatively small campus everyone knows everyone else so that you can't really hide anything. Generally the campus is fairly quiet — no passionate crusades. People get excited about some things — certainly about Kent State and Cambodia — and it's OK to get excited. So far as life at the college goes, there isn't much for students to complain about. Students are involved in just about everything they want to be; they don't feel hassled by anyone; the faculty members are interested and tolerant and are quite willing to give extra time to offering special courses of interest to students. A new system of campus governance involves students, faculty, administration, trustees, and others all working together." That is Carleton — from a conversation with students.

Following the Cambodia and Kent State activities on the campus, Wooster identified what it called "focus groups." These were discussion seminars organized around a whole variety of contemporary social, political, and international issues, and in total they were described as the "new school."

At Susquehanna I was told that about two-thirds of the students had been active in distributing leaflets and other materials in the nearby communities and that there were a good many on-campus teach-ins during the Vietnam moratorium. Although there was further evidence of deep concern following the Cambodia and Kent State events, there was also a fairly clear desire among the students to have classes meet as usual. Last year a fairly large student delegation congregated outside the president's office, but it turned out that it was mainly to compliment the president and sing happy birthday to him. The dean of women said that the students had just recently had a panty raid in the dormitories. Apparently it was set up as a gag.

The following notes come from what I saw and heard at several different campuses: "There was a protest about visiting hours in the dormitories, but for the most part student activity is fairly diversified rather than coalescing around some campuswide matter. They (the administration) busted two students last year for not leaving women's rooms when told." Some administrators made a particular point to tell me that there had been no student uprisings on their campus, a fact that they reported with some pride and satisfaction. "There really isn't much to do here, and no place to go." There is one old theater near the town square. The only eating places are some hamburger and pancake houses. "Sure, students are concerned about what's going on around the world, but efforts to generate support for some cause attain only moderate success because students just aren't that involved."

Religion

"In the early days there was a weekly chapel and attendance was required. As the college grew in enrollment, the chapel was not large enough to seat all the students, so half the students were required to go one week and the other half to go the next week. As the college grew still larger this was changed to every third week, and then to four times a year. Then it was made optional for seniors. Then it was made optional for upperclassmen. Now it is required only for freshmen. There are also Sunday services in the chapel. After the first few Sundays the regular attendance shakes down to about 50 to 80 students—in an auditorium seating 500. The exception is Parents' Weekend. There are two of these a year. On those weekends the chapel is so crowded that they have to have two services."

The Weyerhauser chapel at Macalester is a rather handsome roundish building of wood and glass and is apparently used for a variety of purposes, including music, theater, poetry readings, rock concerts, and discussions, as well as religious services. The chaplain felt that there was not a great deal of interest in formal church services but that there was considerable interest in the personal experience and meaning of religion. Mrs. Weyerhauser had expressed an interest in constructing a chapel for the college some years ago, but it was not until several years later that the college acted on her proposal.

At Wooster the department of religion offers a course on the church in the city for students in the urban studies program. The new chapel at Wooster, designed by Victor Christ-Janer, is primarily a gift of Foster A. McGaw.

A picture of the chapel has been the traditional symbol of Denison college—used on its publications, stationery, etc. I was told that new stationery, without a picture of the chapel, had been ordered.

The large chapel and auditorium at Susquehanna, paid for mainly by the church, seats about 1,500 people. Susquehanna's enrollment is about 1,400.

Money

Carleton was engaged in a 10-year fund drive for $44 million. The drive was in its fourth year and was about on schedule. There is, of course, a continuing need to find money for scholarships and for special purposes.

Macalester has devoted particular attention to making the college attractive for faculty members and to recruiting high-quality students. But they have also spent some of their capital reserves to meet current deficits. From conversations with the officer in charge of the college's financial affairs, I gathered that Macalester overspent its budget last year by about 10 percent. Also, the college has been receiving about a million dollars a year of "soft money," which, of course, may or may not continue indefinitely. Considering their overspending and their current (1970) dependence on soft money, it seemed to me that Macalester could face a

10 to 20 percent belt-tightening process over the next few years. In fact, the trustees had just instructed the chief financial officer to begin that process.

A year or two ago Beloit got a gift of about a million dollars that it used to wipe out accumulated deficits.

The following example illustrates a general problem for many of these schools. A certain family had been a major benefactor of a particular college. The grandchildren, now adults, ultraconservative politically and upset about the behavior of college students, will give no further money to the institution. Will the college try to do things that please this family in order to get its money? The problem is a bit like categorical grants from the government—if you want the money, then you do what the government will pay for.

Goshen college is owned by the Mennonite Board of Education, which in turn appoints the board of overseers for the college. The church is also the major source of funds for the college, with alumni contributions an additional major support.

Wooster has a very high proportion of annual giving among its former students. In fact, it received an award a year ago for having the best record of alumni giving among colleges of its type.

For other colleges, alumni support is at best a minor element, either because they do not have many alumni or because most of their alumni do not have much money. I should imagine this would be true of Susquehanna and Lycoming. Susquehanna's enrollment has grown from 400 to 1,400 within the last 15 years. Lycoming was initially a two-year college and became a four-year college only in 1947. Moreover, teacher training is a major program at both colleges and teaching is not an occupation noted for its economic rewards. The Lutheran Synod has given substantial aid to Susquehanna. Lycoming, although until very recently owned by the Preachers Aid Society, receives little money from the Methodist church. Although I did not get comparable information at each college I visited, it is correct to state that only Goshen got a regular and substantial sum of money from its sponsoring church, and that only at Susquehanna was there any mention of receiving a major sum from the church for some special purpose.

A couple of years ago Pepperdine College started a campaign to raise about $24 million. They got it—including a $2 million property in Malibu where a new campus is being built. The present campus will also be continued. Recently they announced a new campaign for an additional $38 million.

My impression is that the Churches of Christ are very independent, autonomous congregations, without the central or national church organization that is characteristic of the Methodists, Presbyterians, and other mainline denominations. One Church of Christ institution, Harding College in Searcy, Arkansas, has produced a series of films on Americanism that I believe has been highly commended by, among others, officials of the American Legion and the John Birch Society. Pepperdine, another Church of Christ college, was offered a million dollars a few years ago by one of the wealthiest men in Texas if the college would give an honorary degree to a friend of his. Pepperdine said no thank you. But Pepperdine's fund-raising activities have produced several gifts of over a million dollars, including a recent one of about $4 million. At $2 million apiece it would take only 19 contributions to produce $38 million!

Confirmations

There are, I believe, many points of confirmation between the impressions gained from visiting the campuses and the generalizations drawn from analyzing the questionnaire data.

Certainly the friendly atmosphere of the campuses is one such confirmation. While walking across the campuses with the president, or with one of the deans, or with a faculty member, there would inevitably be pauses to say hello to students and colleagues. At one college a dean said to me that a spirit of friendliness was really pervasive on the campus and, partly for that reason, he really likes working there. At several colleges people told me that one of the main virtues of the place was its basic humanism, by which they meant a concern for the individual.

In the chapter on the environment I described a combination of responses that seemed to suggest low energy, low exposure, and low commitment. Arriving at one college about 10 A.M. during the first week of school, I walked past several fraternity houses where there were small groups of men sitting on the porch and a few others lazily tossing a football back and forth on the front lawn. At another college several faculty and staff members felt that the students were generally apathetic. In a conversation with two students at one of the colleges, I was told that there was not a great deal of student activity on the campus and that they felt there was relatively little to do. The reported lack of student demonstrations at several of the colleges was an added confirmation.

One of the educational benefits claimed by students at the

evangelical-fundamentalist colleges to a much greater extent than at other colleges was "vocational training—skills and techniques directly applicable to a job." At Goshen I learned that about half the students go into the field of education, that next in attractiveness was the field of nursing, a program with about 180 students, and that about 120 students were in programs of social work.

The satisfaction with which I was sometimes told about the absence of student demonstrations seemed to reflect a sense of relief that "our students" are not being corrupted by "those radical groups." The political conservatism at some of the colleges was further reflected in their fund-raising activities. At one college a staff member described himself as "the house liberal."

THOUGHTS *On piety and politics*

The 1970 census confirmed the rapid growth of what we might call the Southern tier of the country. There is a major population axis from Miami to Los Angeles, taking in such major (or fast-growing) cities as Atlanta, Birmingham, New Orleans, Memphis, Houston, Dallas and Fort Worth, Oklahoma City, Phoenix, and San Diego. The rising affluence and strength of this Southern tier, along with its rapid population growth, puts it in a position to rival and perhaps to outstrip the historical dominance of the great population centers in the Northern tier of the country, mainly from New York to Chicago, including Philadelphia and Boston, Pittsburgh and Buffalo, Cleveland and Detroit. Both politically and religiously, the Southern tier has usually been described as conservative. Its major religions are more fundamentalist, evangelical, and revivalist than the more formal or liberal religions that dominate the Northern tier. The Bible Belt runs through the South as well as the Midwest. Much of the new wealth of this Southern tier is aggressive and speculative (aerospace, oil, and land) just as in the nineteenth century the aggressive and speculative exploitation of coal and steel built much of the industrial complex from New York to Chicago. The virtues of free enterprise are clearly visible in the new skyscrapers and subdivisions. So, granted this oversimplification may have some validity, one might think that the Southern confluence of patriotism and piety and ecomomic and political power makes a strong bid for national supremacy, and that the country is moving toward a conservative conversion.

Some of the evangelical or fundamentalist colleges might expect major gifts from politically conservative multimillionaires in Texas, Oklahoma, and Southern California. Indeed such gifts have already been made, and the givers are not solely from the Southern tier. In a sense, the fundamentalist colleges exemplify the "American Way"—hard work, individualism, piety, upward mobility, morality, and reward for one's virtue both on earth and in heaven. But much of that "mythology" is part of the civil religion of America and thus has a broader base than evangelical or fundamentalist doctrines. It is nevertheless true that some Protestant colleges have made deliberate efforts to attract gifts from politically conservative (and ultraconservative) sources. At the same time one must add that many evangelical colleges are just not concerned about politics.

I personally do not think that the country is moving toward a conservative conversion and I rather doubt that a great many Protestant colleges will be "saved" either by their piety or by their politics.

On education and evangelism
There is a group of colleges, generally well known, which, although originally Protestant, are now largely if not totally independent. Some maintain a cooperative relationship with the church, but none of them is dependent on it for money or for students. Their present reputation is owing not to their religious activities or affiliations, but rather to the character and quality of their educational programs. Their students come from all parts of the country, or at least from areas well beyond the local region. They are known for the high quality of their student body and for the general goodness of their liberal education and their faculty. They enjoy reasonably good support from alumni, from other donors, and from foundations. They are colleges, in other words, that have made it educationally. Carleton is a good example, as are Macalester and Wooster, among the ones we visited, and so would be, I am sure, such places as Antioch, Oberlin, Swarthmore, Earlham, Pomona, and numerous others. In many ways these colleges stand in contrast to the evangelical-fundamentalist colleges. The kinds of influence they exert, at least as reflected in the interests, attitudes, values, and educational benefits claimed by their students and alumni, are often sharply different from the impact of the more conservative and religiously oriented colleges. They have a fairly dependable clientele and substantially more applicants than they can accommodate; but to maintain their educational quality they need more money, es-

pecially because of rising costs, general inflation, and, owing to the current depression of the economy, lower income from investments, alumni, and other donors.

We think these colleges will survive and, we hope, prosper. Some reasons for this optimism will be noted shortly. Meanwhile, we think the strongly evangelical and fundamentalist colleges will also survive and perhaps prosper, because they too have a dependable clientele, a mission in which they have attained a reputation for success, and a segment of the society, including at least some very wealthy patrons, as well as dedicated evangelicals, determined to guarantee their continued influence.

There is, in addition, a third group of Protestant colleges—colleges that have neither a national reputation based on educational programs nor any strong support from the churches. Their clientele is primarily local and regional rather than national. For the most part they are not tuned in to great wealth or to great zeal. Some of them have what I described as tepid environments—neither warmly spiritual nor coolly intellectual. How many of them will survive depends partly on how much sympathy they can engender, how much public and private support they can rally to that sympathy, and whether the general direction of value changes in society includes a concern for their survival. We need to recall, at this point, that some of these colleges are more like the independent colleges than they are like the fundamentalist colleges.

On the future

A preview of Jean-François Revel's book, *Without Marx or Jesus: The New American Revolution Has Begun,* appeared in the *Saturday Review* dated July 24, 1971. Much of what is discussed there is similar to certain thoughts that have been expressed less comprehensively by social critics in America, and even by persons who hardly qualify as professional critics, but who, in their individual ways, sense that the times are more turbulent than they seemed to be a decade or so ago. There is, I believe, a growing concern about the quality of life, about personal development and better interpersonal relations, about directing technology to more humane ends, and about valuing individuality and experience.

In the *Saturday Review* article, the issues in what is described as America's insurrections against itself are believed to form a cohesive and coherent whole, each issue gaining strength from its relation to other issues. It may be of some relevance to note the extent to which our data from various Protestant colleges and their students make connection with the issues in this presumed revolution.

1. A radically new approach to moral values. This refers to greater permissiveness and openness to varieties of human experience. There is not much help here from Protestant colleges. The fundamentalist colleges are more likely to condone censorship and to uphold a firm division between right and wrong in morality. Students in the more independent colleges are more open to novelty, complexity, and autonomy.

2. The black revolt and

3. The acceptance of guilt for poverty. In our data the acceptance of guilt for racism, prejudice, and poverty was greater among the Protestant-independent college students than among the fundamentalist ones.

4. A growing demand for equality. This is surely related to the previous issues. Students at the Protestant-independent colleges were more supportive of spending money to help right the balance of past inequality.

5. The feminist attack on masculine domination. Again, there seems to be little recognition or support for this issue—at least not as of 1969 when our questionnaires were answered. Among all the Protestant college students, the evangelical-fundamentalist students were the most traditional in their attitudes toward the role of women.

6. Rejection by young people of exclusively economic and technological social goals. We noted that the educational benefits toward which the greatest proportions of students at all our colleges felt they were making most progress were personal and interpersonal insights—personal development, tolerance, appreciation of individuality, social development, and friendships. Science and economic status were much further down the list.

7. Adoption of noncoercive methods in education. Our data on this matter do not permit comparisons among groups. We did note in our visits that nongraded courses, student-initiated courses, and fuller participation in campus governance were evident at some of the colleges.

8. Rejection of an authoritarian culture in favor of a critical and diversified culture. Perhaps we could alter the language of this issue, referring instead to a national or dominant culture and to diversified and regional cultures. The students were supportive of social trends toward greater expressiveness, and felt that they were gaining an appreciation of other cultures and ways of life. Students at the Protestant-independent colleges were engaged in notably more activities related to intercultural affairs, and to art, literature, and drama than were students at the more evangelical or fundamentalist colleges.

9. Rejection of the spread of American power abroad and of foreign policy. Students at the Protestant-independent colleges most clearly rejected the

traditional nationalistic policy of peace through superior strength. They were also least favorable to the trend for business to become more international in scope.

10 Determination that the natural environment is more important than commercial profit. Our survey didn't really bear on this issue. We did find that many of the attitudes, both of students and of alumni, were pro-business, pro-competition, and anti-regulation. At the same time most of them thought it would be desirable if major industries regarded natural resources as belonging to all of society, not just to the owners.

If these are issues around which current debates and dissents in our culture revolve, and if the revolutionary direction of the dissent is correctly perceived, then the evangelical-fundamentalist colleges are outside the mainstream of social change in most cases. But the more independent colleges are in the mainstream of social change at numerous points. In more ways than not, the in-between colleges are closer to the independent colleges than to the evangelical colleges and to that extent they may share in a common future.

A more diversified culture, a more humane regard for independence and individuality, a greater sense of tolerance, a freer social criticism — if these are among the directions of social change, then the educationally strong liberal arts colleges, as exemplars and purveyors of these values, should be the beneficiaries of change. Together with some awakening of the spirit, and with a respect for experience and meaning that comes from both heaven and earth, our society may ensure the diversity of its education, the plurality of its culture, and the Christian part of its heritage.

References

Alumni Survey, Center for the Study of Evaluation, University of California, Los Angeles, 1969. (A questionnaire.)

Barkman, Paul F., Edward R. Dayton, and Edward L. Gruman: *Christian Collegians and Foreign Missions,* Missions Advanced Research and Communication Center, Monrovia, Calif., 1969.

College Student Survey: Upperclassmen, Center for the Study of Evaluation, University of California, Los Angeles, 1969. (A questionnaire.)

"The Jesus Revolution," *Time,* pp. 56–63, June 21, 1971.

Orr, J. Edwin: *Evangelical Awakenings in Collegiate Communities,* University of California, Los Angeles, 1971. (Ed. D. dissertation.)

Pace, C. Robert: *Analysis of a National Sample of College Environments, Final Report of USOE Project No. 5-0764.* Contract No. OE-5-1-321, June 1967.

Pace, C. Robert: *College and University Environment Scales,* Educational Testing Service, Princeton, N.J., Form 1 and Technical Manual, 1963; Form 2 and Technical Manual, 1969a.

Pace, C. Robert: "An Evaluation of Higher Education: Plans and Perspectives," *Journal of Higher Education,* vol. 40, no. 9, December 1969b.

Pattillo, Manning M., Jr., and Donald M. MacKenzie: *Church-Sponsored Higher Education in the United States: Report of the Danforth Commission,* American Council on Education, Washington, D.C., 1966.

"Religion in America," *Daedalus,* vol. 96, no. 1 of the Proceedings of the American Academy of Arts and Sciences, Winter 1967.

Revel, Jean-Francois: "Without Marx or Jesus," *Saturday Review,* vol. 54, no. 30, pp. 14–31, July 24, 1971.

Appendix A: CUES

The following 100 statements, reproduced from CUES (1969a), were used to determine the college's "environment" scores. The statements are grouped under the "scales" to which they belong. The "keyed" response is always TRUE, except as indicated by an asterisk before statements that were keyed FALSE.

Scholarship

The professors really push the students' capacities to the limit.

Most of the professors are dedicated scholars in their fields.

Most courses require intensive study and preparation out of class.

Students set high standards of achievement for themselves.

Class discussions are typically vigorous and intense.

*A lecture by an outstanding scientist would be poorly attended.

Careful reasoning and clear logic are valued most highly in grading student papers, reports, or discussions.

*It is fairly easy to pass most courses without working very hard.

The school is outstanding for the emphasis and support it gives to pure scholarship and basic research.

*Standards set by the professors are not particularly hard to achieve.

Most of the professors are very thorough teachers and really probe into the fundamentals of their subjects.

Most courses are a real intellectual challenge.

Students put a lot of energy into everything they do in class and out.

Course offerings and faculty in the natural sciences are outstanding.

Courses, examinations, and readings are frequently revised.

*Personality, pull, and bluff get students through many courses.

*There is very little studying here over the weekends.

There is a lot of interest in the philosophy and methods of science.

People around here seem to thrive on difficulty—the tougher things get, the harder they work.

Students are very serious and purposeful about their work.

Awareness

Channels for expressing students' complaints are readily accessible.

Students are encouraged to take an active part in social reforms or political programs.

Students are actively concerned about national and international affairs.

There are a good many colorful and controversial figures on the faculty.

There is considerable interest in the analysis of value systems, and the relativity of societies and ethics.

Public debates are held frequently.

A controversial speaker always stirs up a lot of student discussion.

There are many facilities and opportunities for individual creative activity.

There is a lot of interest here in poetry, music, painting, sculpture, architecture, etc.

Concerts and art exhibits always draw big crowds of students.

Students are encouraged to criticize administrative policies and teaching practices.

*The expression of strong personal belief or conviction is pretty rare around here.

Many students here develop a strong sense of responsibility about their role in contemporary social and political life.

There are a number of prominent faculty members who play a significant role in national or local politics.

There would be a capacity audience for a lecture by an outstanding philosopher or theologian.

Course offerings and faculty in the social sciences are outstanding.

Many famous people are brought to the campus for lectures, concerts, student discussions, etc.

The school offers many opportunities for students to understand and criticize important works of art, music, and drama.

Special museums or collections are important possessions of the college.

*Modern art and music get little attention here.

Community

Students often run errands or do other personal services for the faculty.

The history and traditions of the college are strongly emphasized.

The professors go out of their way to help you.

There is a great deal of borrowing and sharing among the students.

When students run a project or put on a show everybody knows about it.

Many upperclassmen play an active role in helping new students adjust to campus life.

Students exert considerable pressure on one another to live up to the expected codes of conduct.

*Graduation is a pretty matter-of-fact, unemotional event.

It is easy to take clear notes in most courses.

The school helps everyone get acquainted.

This school has a reputation for being very friendly.

All undergraduates must live in university approved housing.

Instructors clearly explain the goals and purposes of their courses.

Students have many opportunities to develop skill in organizing and directing the work of others.

*Most of the faculty are not interested in students' personal problems.

Students quickly learn what is done and not done on this campus.

It's easy to get a group together for card games, singing, going to the movies, etc.

Students commonly share their problems.

*Faculty members rarely or never call students by their first names.

There is a lot of group spirit.

Propriety

*Many students drive sports cars.

*Students frequently do things on the spur of the moment.

Student publications never lampoon dignified people or institutions.

*The person who is always trying to "help out" is likely to be regarded as a nuisance.

Students are conscientious about taking good care of school property.

Students are expected to report any violation of rules and regulations.

*Student parties are colorful and lively.

*There always seem to be a lot of little quarrels going on.

Students rarely get drunk and disorderly.

Most students show a good deal of caution and self-control in their behavior.

*Bermuda shorts, pin-up pictures, etc., are common on this campus.

*Students pay little attention to rules and regulations.

Dormitory raids, water fights, and other student pranks would be unthinkable.

*Many students seem to expect other people to adapt to them rather than trying to adapt themselves to others.

*Rough games and contact sports are an important part of intramural athletics.

Students ask permission before deviating from common policies or practices.

*Most student rooms are pretty messy.

*People here are always trying to win an argument.

*Drinking and late parties are generally tolerated, despite regulations.

*Students occasionally plot some sort of escapade or rebellion.

Practicality

Students almost always wait to be called on before speaking in class.

The big college events draw a lot of student enthusiasm and support.

There is a recognized group of student leaders on this campus.

Frequent tests are given in most courses.

*Student pep rallies, parades, dances, carnivals, or demonstrations occur very rarely.

Anyone who knows the right people in the faculty or administration can get a better break here.

The important people at this school expect others to show proper respect for them.

Student elections generate a lot of intense campaigning and strong feeling.

Everyone has a lot of fun at this school.

In many classes students have an assigned seat.

Student organizations are closely supervised to guard against mistakes.

Many students try to pattern themselves after people they admire.

New fads and phrases are continually springing up among the students.

Students must have a written excuse for absence from class.

The college offers many really practical courses such as typing, report writing, etc.

Student rooms are more likely to be decorated with pennants and pin-ups than with paintings, carvings, mobiles, fabrics, etc.

Students take a great deal of pride in their personal appearance.

Education here tends to make students more practical and realistic.

The professors regularly check up on the students to make sure that assignments are being carried out properly and on time.

It's important socially here to be in the right club or group.

Appendix B: Activity Scales from the Alumni Survey Questionnaire

COMMUNITY AFFAIRS

During the past year:

_____ I talked about local community problems with my friends.

_____ I followed local events regularly in my newspaper.

_____ I gave money to the community fund or chest or other local charity.

_____ I belonged to a community organization interested in civic affairs—such as PTA, Chamber of Commerce, League of Women Voters, business or professional association, etc.

_____ I attended meetings of some local civic group.

_____ I contributed time or money to some civic project—such as a playground, park, school, hospital, museum, theater, etc.

_____ I had contact with a local official about some community problem.

_____ I collected money, called on my neighbors, carried a petition, or engaged in some similar activity in behalf of a local community project.

_____ I voted in the last local election.

_____ I attended a public hearing about a local issue—such as zoning, schools, taxes, traffic, etc.

_____ I participated in a demonstration or protest about a local issue.

_____ I held office in some local civic group or community organization.

NATIONAL AND STATE POLITICS

During the past year:

_____ I discussed political issues with my friends.

_____ I listened to speeches, news specials, discussion programs, etc. about political issues on TV or radio weekly or monthly.

_____ I followed state and national political events regularly in my newspaper.

_____ I read magazine articles about state and national problems weekly or monthly.

_____ I read one or more books about politics.

_____ I voted in the last national election.

_____ I voted in the last state election.

_____ I attended meetings of a political club or group.

_____ I did some volunteer or paid work for a political party.

_____ I contributed money to some political cause or group.

_____ I talked with an elected official about some problem (national or state).

_____ I signed a petition, wrote a letter, card, or telegram concerned with some political issue.

_____ I participated in a public protest or rally over some political issue.

_____ I held a political or public office (elected or appointed, full time or part time).

ART

During the past year:

_____ I talked about art with my friends.
_____ I read critiques or reviews of art shows or exhibits in the newspapers or magazines.
_____ I visited an art gallery or art museum.
_____ I attended an exhibition of contemporary painting or sculpture.
_____ I read one or more books about art, artists, or art history.
_____ I bought a painting or piece of sculpture.
_____ I attended an art study group or workshop.
_____ I contributed money or time in support of some activity related to art.
_____ I did some creative painting or other art work myself.

LITERATURE

During the past year:

_____ I talked about new books with my friends.
_____ I read book reviews in the newspapers or magazines at least once a month.
_____ I read for personal interest (not business) at least one book a month.
_____ I bought books for my personal library.
_____ I read one or more contemporary novels.
_____ I read poetry.
_____ I attended a lecture given by a novelist, critic, poet, or playwright.
_____ I belonged to a group which discussed books.
_____ I wrote an essay, story, play, poem, etc., for publication.

EDUCATION

During the past year:

_____ I talked with my friends about the schools in the neighborhood.
_____ I visited a local school.
_____ I talked with a school teacher or other school official.
_____ I read about education in the newspaper.
_____ I voted (or would vote) in favor of a bond issue or other proposition to provide more money for the public schools.
_____ I enrolled in a course offered by a college or university.
_____ I attended one or more concerts or lectures at a college or university campus.
_____ I attended one or more athletic events at a college or university.
_____ I gave money to a college or university.
_____ I read one or more books about education.

MUSIC

During the past year:

_____ I bought phonograph records.
_____ I listened attentively to radio music at home or in my car.
_____ I read reviews of musical performances or new record releases in the newspapers or magazines.
_____ I talked about music with my friends.
_____ I attended one or more symphony, opera, or chamber music concerts.
_____ I attended one or more concerts of contemporary folk music, rock, jazz, etc.
_____ I read one or more books about music, musicians, or music history.
_____ I listened to some serious music by contemporary composers.

_____ I contributed time or money in support of some local musical enterprise.
_____ I played a musical instrument.
_____ I participated in some vocal or instrumental group—choir, orchestra, or other group.

DRAMA

During the past year:

_____ I talked about movies, plays, TV dramas, etc. with my friends.
_____ I watched TV dramas at least once a month.
_____ I went to the movies at least once a month.
_____ I read theater or movie reviews in the newspapers or magazines at least once a month.
_____ I read one or more books about the theater, or a book of plays.
_____ I attended one or more plays—either professional or amateur.
_____ I belonged to a group which discussed contemporary drama.
_____ I attended one or more plays by a contemporary dramatist.
_____ I saw several movies that could be described as experimental, avant garde, etc.
_____ I contributed time or money in support of some local theatrical enterprise.
_____ I participated in some drama activity—acted, danced, sang, worked on sets or costumes, made movies, etc.

RELIGION

During the past year:

_____ I attended church services one or more times.
_____ I belonged to a church.
_____ I contributed a regular sum of money to the church.
_____ I read articles about church or religious activities in the newspapers or magazines.
_____ I read one or more books about religion.
_____ I attended one or more church functions held during the week.
_____ I did some volunteer work for my church.
_____ I discussed ideas, practices, or problems of religion with my friends.
_____ I observed religious rituals in my home (said grace before meals, lit candles on the Sabbath, etc.).

INTERCULTURAL

During the past year:

_____ I talked with my friends about people and cultural events in other countries.
_____ I saw one or more foreign movies.
_____ I went to a concert, theater, or exhibition which featured the art, music, or drama of another country.
_____ I corresponded with a citizen of another country.
_____ I traveled in another country.
_____ I entertained a visitor from another country.
_____ I read one or more books by authors from another country.
_____ I attended one or more meetings or lectures about other countries or about other racial or ethnic groups.
_____ I participated in efforts to improve understanding between countries, races, or ethnic groups.
_____ I attended a meeting at which a large majority of the participants were of a racial background different from mine. (If so, what was the racial background of most of the participants? Underline one: Black, Brown, Yellow, White, Other.)

SCIENCE

During the past year:

_____ I talked about science with my friends.
_____ I watched special presentations about science on TV.
_____ I read articles about new developments in scientific research in the newspapers or magazines.
_____ I attended a scientific exhibit or museum.
_____ I read a new book about science.
_____ I subscribed to a magazine about science.
_____ I attended a lecture or demonstration on some aspect of science.
_____ I attended meetings of a science study club or work group.
_____ I carried out a scientific experiment, recorded scientific observations of things in the natural setting, or assembled and maintained a collection of scientific specimens.
_____ I made some piece of scientific apparatus—such as a hi-fi component, photo-enlarger, telescope, etc.

INTERNATIONAL

During the past year:

_____ I discussed international relations, foreign policy, the U. N. etc., with my friends.
_____ I read newspapers or magazine articles dealing with international relations.
_____ I read one or more books about other countries or international relations.
_____ I read U.N. publications or listened to U.N. sponsored programs on radio or TV.
_____ I contributed time or money for some international group or project.
_____ I spoke to a civic group or club on international relations or foreign policy.
_____ I attended one or more meetings or lectures about international affairs or foreign policy.
_____ I wrote to a news publication or government official in behalf of some legislation or U.S. policy regarding international relations.
_____ I participated in a public demonstration for or against some international issue.

Index

Albion College, 34, 95, 97
Allegheny College, 34
Alma College, 34
American Legion, 102
Amherst College, 11
Anderson College, 14, 33
Antioch College, 11, 104
Asbury College, 14
Atlantic Christian College, 34
Augustana College, 33
Austin College, 33
Azusa Pacific College, 14

Baldwin-Wallace College, 11
Barrington College, 33
Baylor University, 2, 14
Beecher, Lyman, 10
Beloit College, 34, 40, 95, 97, 101
Bethel College and Seminary (St. Paul, Minnesota), 14
Birmingham Southern College, 34
Blackburn College, 34
Bluffton College, 34
Boston University, 2
Bridgewater College, 33
Brown University (formerly Rhode Island College), 10

California, University of:
 at Berkeley, 14, 28
 at Los Angeles, 14
  Center for the Study of Evaluation, Graduate School of Education, 3

California Institute of Technology, 15
Carleton College, 95, 97, 98, 100, 104
Carnegie Commission on Higher Education, 3
Carthage College, 34
Chicago, University of, 2, 14
Christ-Janer, Victor, 100
Coe College, 34
Colby College, 40
Colgate University, 40
College and University Environment Scales (CUES), 3, 6, 17–18, 27–28, 33, 45, 56
Columbia College, 33
Concordia College, 33, 74, 80
Congregational Church (Charlestown, Massachusetts), 9
Cornell College, 34
CUES (*see* College and University Environment Scales)

Danforth Foundation, 1, 33
Dartmouth College, 10, 11
Denison University, 11, 34, 73, 95, 97, 98, 100
Drew University, 73
Duke University, 2
Dwight, Timothy, 10, 11

Earlham College, 34, 40, 104
Eastern Baptist College, 34
Eastern Mennonite College, 33
Elizabethtown College, 34

121

Erskine College, 33
Evansville College, 34

Findlay College, 34
Fort Wayne Bible College, 14
Franklin University, 11, 34, 95, 96

George Fox College, 33
Gordon College, 33
Goshen College, 33, 74, 95–97, 101, 103
Graham, William Franklin (Billy), 1, 13–14
Greenville College, 34
Guilford College, 34
Gustavus Adolphus College, 34

Hanover College, 34
Harding College, 102
Harvard, John, 1, 9
Heidelberg College, 11
Hiram College, 11
Hobart College, 34, 40
Huntington College, 33

Illinois Wesleyan University, 34
Indiana Central College, 34

Jackson State College, 28
Jefferson, Thomas, 10
John Birch Society, 102
Jones, Dr. E. Stanley, 13
Jones, Griffith, 9
Judson College, 34

Kalamazoo College, 34
Kent State University, 28, 98, 99
Kenyon College, 11
Keuka College, 34
King's College (now Columbia University), 9

Lafayette College, 34
Lambuth College, 33
Lewis and Clark College, 33

Lindenwood College for Women, 34
Luther College, 34
Lycoming College, 34, 95, 96, 101
Lynchburg College, 34

Macalester College, 34, 95–97, 100, 104
   Weyerhauser Chapel, 100
McGaw, Foster, 100
MacKenzie, Donald M., 1, 33
Madison, Bishop James, 11
Malone College, 34
Manchester College, 34
Marshall, Chief Justice John, 11
Maryville College, 34
Massachusetts Institute of Technology, 15
Mennonite Board of Education, 101
Meredith College, 33
Messiah College, 33
Methodist College, 2
Michigan, University of, 12, 14, 28
   Student Christian Association, 12
Millikin University, 34
Minnesota, University of, 14
Moravian College, 34
Mount Union College, 11
Muskingum College, 11

New Jersey, College of, 9
North Carolina, University of, 14
Northland College, 34
Northwestern University, 2, 14

Oberlin College, 11, 104
Ohio Northern University, 33
Ohio State University, 14
Ohio Wesleyan University, 11
Oklahoma Baptist University, 34
Oral Roberts University, 14
Orr, J. Edwin, 9n.
Ottawa University, 34
Otterbein College, 11

Paine, Thomas, 10
Pasadena College, 33
Pattillo, Manning M., Jr., 1, 33

Pennsylvania, University of, 9
Pepperdine College, 74, 101, 102
Philander Smith College, 34
Pomona College, 104
Preachers Aid Society, 101
Presbyterian College, 2
Princeton University, 10, 11, 26
Puget Sound, University of, 34

Queens College (now Rutgers University), 10

Randolph Macon Woman's College, 34
Revel, Jean-François, 105
Rhode Island College (now Brown University), 10
Roberts, Evan, 13
Rollins College, 40

San Francisco State College, 28
Seattle Pacific College, 14, 34
Shimer College, 34, 40
Simpson College, 34
Southern California, University of, 2
Southern Methodist University, 2
Southwestern Baptist Seminary, 14
Spring Arbor College, 14
Stanford University, 26, 28
Stetson University, 34
Student Christian Association, University of Michigan, 12
Susquehanna University, 34, 95, 97, 99–101
 Environmental Studies Institute, 97
Swarthmore College, 104
Syracuse University, 2

Taylor University, 14
Tennent, William, 9
Tennessee, University of, 14

Tennessee Wesleyan College, 34
Texas Christian University, 2
Trinity Church (New York City), 9
Tulsa, University of, 34

U.S. Office of Education, National Center for Educational Statistics, 1
Ursinus College, 34

Valparaiso University, 34
Virginia, University of, 12

Wake Forest College, 2
Wallace, DeWitt, 96
Wallace, James, 96
Warner Pacific College, 34
Wayne State University, 26
Waynesburg College, 34
Wesley, John, 9
Western Maryland College, 34
Western Reserve University, 11
Westminster College, 34
Westmont College, 33, 73
Weyerhauser, Mrs. Frederick K., 100
Wheaton College (Illinois), 13–14
Wheaton College (Massachusetts), 14
Whitefield, George, 9
William and Mary, College of, 9
William Smith College, 40
Williams College, 10, 11
Wisconsin, University of, 28
Wittenberg University, 11, 34
Wooster, College of, 34, 95–101, 104
World's Student Christian Federation, 13

Yale University, 10, 11
Young Men's Christian Association (YMCA), 12, 13

This book was set in Vladimir by University Graphics, Inc.
It was printed on acid-free, long-life paper and bound by The
Maple Press Company. The designers were Elliot Epstein and
Edward Butler. The editors were Nancy Tressel and Janine Parson
for McGraw-Hill Book Company and Verne A. Stadtman, Terry Y.
Allen and Sidney J. P. Hollister for the Carnegie Commission on
Higher Education. Alice Cohen supervised the production.